Hisat'sinom

The publication of this volume was made possible in part
by a generous gift from Anthropologist David E. Stuart.

Hisat'sinom
Ancient Peoples in a Land without Water

Edited by Christian E. Downum

A School for Advanced Research Popular Archaeology Book

SAR
PRESS

School for Advanced Research Press
Santa Fe

School for Advanced Research Press
Post Office Box 2188
Santa Fe, New Mexico 87504-2188
www.sarpress.org

Managing Editor: Lisa Pacheco
Editorial Assistant: Ellen Goldberg
Designer and Production Manager: Cynthia Dyer
Manuscript Editor: Jane Kepp
Proofreader: June-el Piper
Indexer: Ina Gravitz
Printed in China by Everbest, Four Colour Print Group

Library of Congress Cataloging-in-Publication Data

Hisatsinom : ancient peoples in a land without water / edited by Christian E. Downum.
   p. cm. -- (School for advanced research popular southwestern archaeology book)
   Includes bibliographical references and index.
   ISBN 978-1-934691-11-3 (alk. paper) -- ISBN 978-1-934691-12-0 (alk. paper)
   1. Sinagua culture. 2. Hohokam culture. 3. Chaco culture. 4. Pueblo Indians. 5. Arizona--Antiquities.
       I. Downum, Christian E. (Christian Eric), 1957-
               E99.S547H57 2011
               979.1'01--dc22
               2011004020

Cover photograph: Michael Collier, Lomaki and the San Francisco peaks. Used with permission.
Frontispiece: Twelfth-century textile petroglyph near Citadel Pueblo. Drawn from photo by Christian E. Downum.

Contents

Color plates follow page 48.

Acknowledgments

Many people deserve thanks for their help in making this book a reality, not least my colleagues who contributed chapters; their outstanding work speaks for itself. I offer great appreciation to the staff of Northern Arizona University's Bilby Research Center, especially the supremely talented photographers Dan Boone and Ryan Belnap, without whose assistance the book would not have been possible. Thanks also to the incomparable Victor O. Leshyk for his exceptional illustrations and designs, which helped bring our vision of the past to life.

At the Museum of Northern Arizona, I thank Robert Breunig and Kelley Hays-Gilpin for their support of the project; Elaine Hughes, Kathleen Dougherty, and Carmen Li for access to collections and assistance with photography; and Jonathan Pringle for assistance with archives and photo collections. At Northern Arizona University's Cline Library, Jess Vogelsang offered assistance with photos from the Colorado Plateau digital archives. At the U.S. National Park Service and Flagstaff Area National Monuments, superintendents Sam Henderson and Diane Chung and staff members including Al Remley, Todd Metzger, Helen Fairley, Gwen Gallenstein, Sue Fischer, Lloyd Masayumptewa, Bernie Natseway, and Lisa Baldwin helped with access to collections and assistance with fieldwork and photography.

I thank Peter J. Pilles Jr. for his generous loan of photographs, access to Elden Pueblo collections, editorial advice, for sharing his knowledge about Sinagua archaeology over the years, and for reading and commenting on the manuscript for the book. Joe Vogel, Bern Carey, Jane Kolber, Bob Mark, Evelyn Billo, and Michael Collier also generously shared photographs and other images. Roger Dorr and Jeremy Haines lent specimens for photography. Laurie Coveney Thom provided administrative assistance throughout the project. Desert Archaeology, Inc., gave permission to reproduce multiple images, and Tom Taylor and the Shooting Star Inn graciously hosted our authors' confab.

At the School for Advanced Research in Santa Fe, I thank the editorial and production staff at SAR Press for all their help and good work, especially Catherine Cocks in the early stages of manuscript development and Lisa Pacheco in the later stages. Thanks to Jane Kepp for her superb editing and advice, and to Press director Lynn Baca for her patience throughout a long project.

Appreciation also goes to the U.S. National Park Service, the Western National Parks Association, the National Science Foundation, the Arizona Department of Transportation, the Arizona State Historic Preservation Office, the University of Arizona Laboratory of Tree-Ring Research, the Coconino National Forest, Grinnell College, the Babbitt Ranches, the Museum of Northern Arizona, and Northern Arizona University for supporting the research that appears in this volume.

Places to Visit in the Sierra Sin Agua

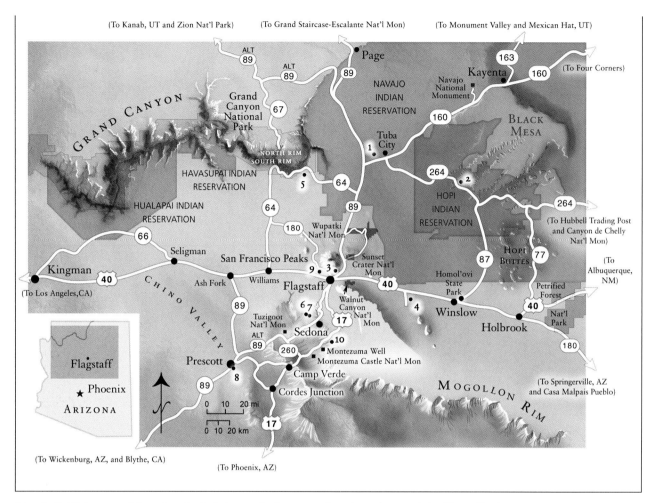

Map 1. Publicly accessible archaeological sites and other attractions in and around the Sierra Sin Agua.

National and State Parks and Monuments

In addition to the places listed here, the two largest, best-known parks in the area are Grand Canyon National Park and Petrified Forest National Park. General contact for nearby national monuments is Headquarters, Flagstaff Area National Monuments, 6400 N. Hwy 89, Flagstaff, AZ 86004, phone (928) 526-1157. Visitors are advised to call ahead if possible and verify operating hours, access, facilities, weather, and permissibility of pets on trails. Visit on the web at www.nps.gov.

Wupatki National Monument encompasses more than 55 square miles of high desert north of Flagstaff, Arizona. The major attraction is Wupatki Pueblo, a multistory, 100-room sandstone building where Native people lived mostly during the 1100s CE. A half-mile round-trip trail leads to the pueblo and its great kiva and ball court. Other ruins, including Wukoki, the Citadel, and Lomaki, are accessible by paved road. There is also a small museum with a bookstore, gift shop, restrooms, and picnic area. Contact the visitor center at (928) 679-2365, fax (928) 679-2349.

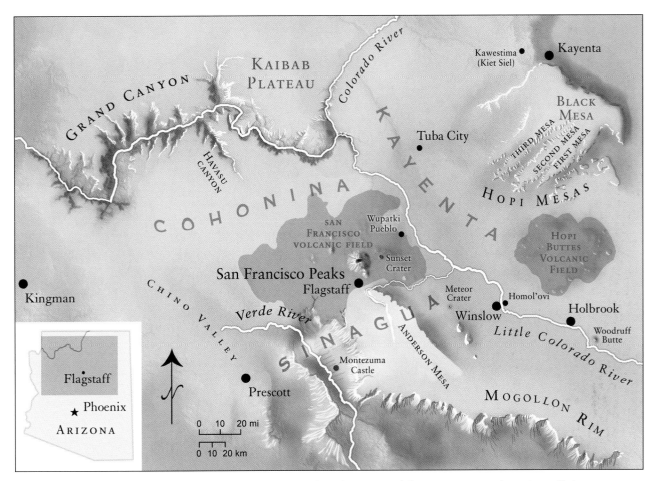

Map 2. Major geographical features, archaeological sites, and modern cities of the region surrounding Flagstaff, Arizona.

Sunset Crater National Monument features Sunset Crater volcano and its surrounding landscape. Short hiking trails lead to lava flows, fumaroles, cinder deposits, and other interesting features associated with the volcano's eruption. A visitor center offers exhibits on regional geology, volcanology, natural history, and archaeology. Contact the visitor center at (928) 526-0502.

Walnut Canyon National Monument preserves and interprets cliff dwellings and open-air sites dating to the 1100s and 1200s. A visitor center, museum, gift shop, and bookstore sit on the north rim of the canyon. A steep hiking trail leads to cliff dwellings built into the canyon walls, and a relatively flat trail leads to pueblo and pit house ruins along the rim of the canyon. Contact the visitor center at (928) 526-3367.

Montezuma Castle National Monument features an erroneously named but beautiful, five-story cliff dwelling—it is not a castle and has no connection to the Aztec leader Montezuma. The monument offers a visitor center with bookstore and museum and a short trail along Beaver Creek below the site. Contact the monument at P.O. Box 219, Camp Verde, AZ 86322, or 527 S. Main St., Camp Verde, AZ 86322; phone (928) 567-3322 (visitor information) or (928) 567-5276 (headquarters); fax (928) 567-3597.

Montezuma Well is a unit of Montezuma Castle National Monument featuring a collapsed limestone cavern fed by a spring that issues more than a million gallons of water a day. The rim of the cavern hosts a small cliff dwelling. A surface pueblo and ancient irrigation canals, hardened with travertine deposits, lie nearby. Phone (928) 567-4521.

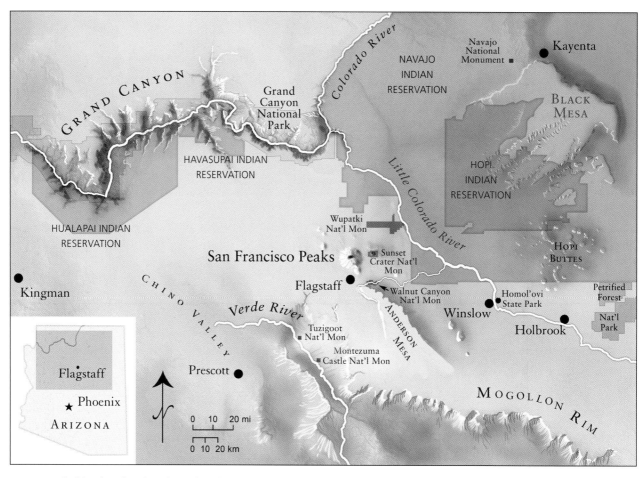

Map 3. Tribal land and archaeological parks and monuments of the region.

Tuzigoot National Monument, along the Verde River near Clarkdale, Arizona, offers visitors a walk through the ruins of a 110-room, hilltop pueblo of the southern Sinagua archaeological culture. A museum with bookstore and gift shop displays ancient artifacts from the ruin. Contact Tuzigoot Visitor Center, P.O. Box 219, Camp Verde, AZ 86322; phone (928) 634-5564 (visitor information) or (928) 567-5276 (headquarters); fax (928) 567-3597.

Homolovi State Park is a 4,000-acre preserve that interprets some large pueblos dating mostly from the 1200s through 1400s CE. Amenities include a visitor center and museum, interpretive trails leading to local ruins, and a campground. Contact Arizona State Parks, 1300 W. Washington St.,

Phoenix, AZ 85007, phone (602) 542-4174, or Homolovi State Park, 928-289-4106.

Navajo National Monument preserves and interprets numerous archaeological sites, but visitor activities are focused on late-thirteenth-century Betatakin and Kiet Siel, two of the Southwest's largest and most spectacularly well-preserved cliff dwellings. Short trails offering an overview of Betatakin are open year-round. Ranger-guided hikes to Betatakin (a 5-mile round trip) take place when weather permits. Kiet Siel (a 17-mile round-trip hike) is accessible only through seasonal tours, for which reservations are required. Contact Superintendent, Navajo National Monument, HC 71 Box 3, Tonalea, AZ 86044, phone (928) 672-2700.

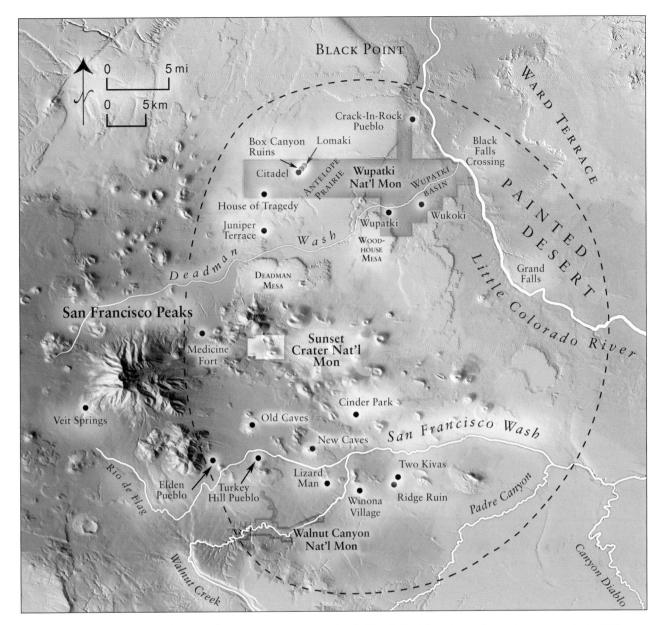

Map 4. Major archaeological places in the Sierra Sin Agua heartland. The dashed line shows the major extent of ash fall from the Sunset Crater Volcano.

Other Places of Interest (Numbered on Map 1)

1. Dinosaur Tracks. This undeveloped site offers visitors a chance to see dinosaur tracks from the Jurassic period, some 200 million years ago. Craft vendors are often present, along with guides who give tours of the tracks for a donation. Nearby Tuba City has lodging, restaurants, and shopping and serves as a gateway to the Navajo Nation, the Hopi Mesas, and points east, including Navajo National Monument and the Four Corners.

2. Hopi Tribal Center. Located on Second Mesa, the Hopi Tribal Center features a cultural museum, hotel, and restaurant for visitors to the Hopi Mesas. The restaurant offers a variety of menu items, including traditional Hopi foods. Phone (928) 734-2401 (hotel reservations) or (928) 734-2402 (restaurant).

3. Elden Pueblo is an interpretive, educational, and research site in the Coconino National Forest along Highway 89 within the city of Flagstaff. Its main feature is a multistory pueblo dating from about

1070 to 1275 CE. The site has no facilities, but short, self-guided tours are available year-round. At times during the summer the public can participate in formal site tours, excavations, and artifact washing and analysis. A summer archaeology camp trains students in third grade and higher. Contact Elden Pueblo Program Manager, P.O. Box 3496, Flagstaff, AZ 86003, phone (928) 527-3452, or Flagstaff Ranger District, 5075 N. Highway 89, Flagstaff, AZ 86004, phone (928) 526-0866.

4. Meteor Crater is a privately owned facility featuring a mile-wide meteorite impact crater that formed about 50,000 years ago. The site offers interpretive trails, a movie theater, an interactive discovery center, a gift shop, and an Astronaut Memorial Park along the crater's rim. The crater is an important landmark to the Hopis and other tribal groups in the area. Contact Meteor Crater Enterprises, P.O. Box 30940, Flagstaff, AZ 86003; phone (928) 289-5898, toll free 800-289-5898; fax (928) 289-2598.

5. Tusayan Ruins is a small, late-twelfth-century pueblo in Grand Canyon National Park that was excavated in the early 1930s. A short interpretive trail winds around pueblo rooms and a kiva. A small museum displays ancient artifacts from the Grand Canyon region, including Archaic-age split-twig figurines, along with contemporary craft items made by local tribes.

6. Honanki Heritage Site, in the famous red rock country just west of Sedona, Arizona, preserves and interprets a multistory cliff dwelling in the Coconino National Forest dating from the 1100s through 1300s. The site offers a small parking lot and short interpretive trail, along with toilets and a small interpretive kiosk. Contact Red Rock Ranger District, P.O. Box 20249, Sedona AZ 86341, phone (928) 282-4119. Commercial tours are available.

7. Palatki Heritage Site, also in the Coconino National Forest, offers two trails, each about one-quarter mile long, leading, respectively, to an alcove

with ancient pictographs and to the Palatki cliff dwelling, a "sister site" to Honanki. Facilities include a parking lot, toilets, water, and a small visitor center and bookstore. Contact Red Rock Ranger District as above. Reservations are recommended because the Coconino National Forest sometimes restricts the number of visitors.

8. Prescott, Arizona, features two museums devoted to local archaeology and Native peoples. The *Smoki Museum* displays ancient artifacts from northern and central Arizona along with dioramas of ancient life and contemporary Native American craft items, including jewelry, baskets, and katsina carvings. Contact Smoki Museum, 147 N. Arizona Ave., P.O. Box 10224, Prescott, AZ 86304-0224, phone (928) 445-1230. The *Sharlot Hall Museum* is devoted primarily to Arizona history but also features ethnographic materials from local tribes. Contact Sharlot Hall Museum, 415 W. Gurley St., Prescott AZ 86301, phone (928) 445-3122.

9. The Museum of Northern Arizona, on Highway 180 on the west side of Flagstaff, is a pioneering institution in the archaeology, ethnology, and natural history of the Colorado Plateau. Its five permanent and three changing exhibits display items from the museum's holdings of nearly 5 million objects, covering anthropology, biology, geology, and fine art. Its large gift shop offers books, music, clothing, and Native American art and crafts. Address 3101 N. Ft. Valley Rd., Flagstaff, AZ 86001, phone (928) 774-5213.

10. The V-bar-V petroglyph site preserves more than 1,000 petroglyphs, the largest known set of petroglyphs in the Verde Valley. It lies about one-half mile from the interpretive *USFS Visitor Center*. Members of the Verde Valley Archaeological Society and Friends of the Forest provide on-site management and offer guided tours. Contact Red Rock Heritage Sites, P.O. Box 20429, Sedona AZ 86341, phone (928) 282-3854.

A Site Etiquette Guide

The following guidelines come from the Coconino National Forest but are applicable to archaeological sites everywhere in the Southwest.

• Walls are fragile and continue to deteriorate—that's why they're called ruins. Climbing, sitting, or standing on walls and picking up or moving rocks compromises these sites.

• Artifacts, where they lie, tell a story. Once an artifact is moved, a piece of the past is lost forever. Removing artifacts or piling them up at a site destroys the story they can tell.

• Drawing, scratching, carving, painting, and oil from even the cleanest hands can cause deterioration of ancient drawings on rock. Please help the scientists who are trying to unravel the meaning of these symbols by refraining from touching the rock art. Mindless graffiti destroys rock art and is disrespectful to contemporary Native Americans.

• Cultural deposits, including the soil itself on an archaeological site, are important for scientific tests used in reconstructing past environments. Adding anything to a site—even well-intentioned offerings—destroys the potential for such tests.

• Fire destroys prehistoric organic materials and damages rock art by covering it with soot. Absolutely no fires, candles, smudging, or smoking is allowed at sites. Camping is not allowed at Palatki, Honanki, and many other ruins, and is discouraged at all archaeological sites.

• Fragile desert plants and soils that are part of archaeological sites are destroyed when you stray from the trail. You may also disturb the small desert animals that make their homes in the bushes, under rocks, and in burrows. Please stay on the trails—they are there for a reason. Bicycles and motorized vehicles are not allowed beyond the parking lot.

• Animals damage sites by digging, urinating, and defecating in them. They can destroy fragile cultural deposits and frighten other visitors. No pets are allowed in these sites.

Chronology of the Hisat'sinom

Years before present

13,125–12,925	Clovis culture: hunting of large game such as mammoths and bison
12,925–9,000	Later Paleoindians: initial focus on hunting of bison; later, transition to more varied hunting and gathering
9,000–6,200	Early Archaic
6,200–4,600	Middle Archaic
4,600–1,600	Late Archaic

Dates CE ("of the common era")

200–400	Earliest evidence of maize agriculture in the Sierra Sin Agua
550–825	Earliest evidence of Sinagua and Cohonina settlements, accompanied by distinctive local pottery traditions, life in small hamlets of shallow pit houses
825–1025	Extent of settlement expands; elaboration of Sinagua and Cohonina cultural patterns
About 1068–1080	Eruption of Sunset Crater
1025–1090	Continued expansion of number and extent of settlements; eclectic combination of architectural forms; hamlets concentrated along edges of treeless areas in high-elevation ponderosa pine forests
1090–1140	Construction of 11 ball courts; establishment of extensive pit house settlements such as Winona Village and Ridge Ruin; evidence of Hohokam-like houses, artifacts, architecture, and burial practices
1110–1175	Construction and occupation of Ridge Ruin Pueblo
1130–1140	Cohonina occupation of western San Francisco Peaks ends; use of most ball courts comes to an end
1130s	Serious drought; evidence of violent conflict along cultural frontiers south of the Wupatki area
1137	Major construction of Wupatki Pueblo begins
1140–1220	Time of large pueblos such as Wupatki and Elden, expansion of trade networks, and construction of large open-air plazas, subterranean community rooms, and great kivas
1200s	A notably cold century, with no warm periods and three lengthy cool periods totaling 60 years
1215–1221	Period of sharply reduced precipitation, coming at the end of a 24-year cool interval
1220–1250	Major retraction of settlements; construction at Wupatki ends; Wupatki Basin vacated, as is much of Flagstaff area
1250–1300	Consolidation of remaining settlement in Flagstaff area into large pueblos (Elden and Turkey Hill) or hilltop sites (Old Caves and New Caves Pueblos)
1300–1450	End of settlement in Flagstaff area; construction of large pueblo communities on Anderson Mesa, in Verde Valley, and along Little Colorado River near Winslow
About 1450	Verde Valley, Anderson Mesa, and middle Little Colorado drainage vacated
1539–1540	Spaniards arrive in Southwest
1680	Pueblo Revolt drives Spanish from the northern Southwest until 1692
1830s	Initial Anglo-American exploration of Flagstaff area
1851	Sitgreaves Expedition encounters Wupatki Pueblo
1863–1868	Navajo "Long Walk" and incarceration at Fort Sumner, New Mexico
1880s	Anglo settlement of Flagstaff; arrival of railroad
1915	Walnut Canyon National Monument established
1924	Wupatki National Monument established
1928	Museum of Northern Arizona founded
1930	Sunset Crater National Monument established; Discovery by archaeologists that Sunset Crater erupted during time of human occupation

Hisat'sinom

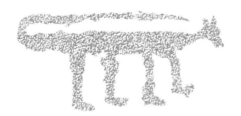

Figure 1.1. The San Francisco Peaks in winter, with the summit, at an elevation of 12,637 feet, shrouded in clouds. The Hopi name for the peaks is Nuvatukya'ovi, "place of the high snows."

Hisat'sinom and the Sierra Sin Agua

Ancient Peoples and Places of the San Francisco Peaks

Christian E. Downum

The landscape surrounding modern Flagstaff, Arizona, is a stunningly beautiful place of extremes, rising from hot desert lowlands to snowcapped mountain peaks. The vegetation is mostly pine forest, piñon-juniper savannah, and grassland, subtly transitioning from one to the other with changes in elevation. More than 600 volcanoes dot the landscape. They include the San Francisco Peaks, a graceful, glacially sculpted mountain that is the highest point in Arizona and perhaps its most revered summit. Around the peaks lies a rough expanse of volcanic debris, chaotically strewn atop neat layers of sedimentary rock. Black, jagged lava flows and reddish brown, cone-shaped volcanoes interrupt deep, undulating cinder dunes. These features remind us of a fiery, violent past and give the land an otherworldly quality.

Everywhere, water is scarce. High elevations often receive abundant winter snows and summer rains, but porous volcanic cinders and fractured sedimentary rocks absorb much of the moisture and keep it from concentrating into bodies of surface water such as rivers and lakes. This circumstance led early Spanish explorers to dub the region "Sierra Sin Agua"—mountains without water.

Despite the aridity, abundant archaeological remains testify to a thriving ancient population. Many of the best-preserved archaeological sites now exist as parks and monuments. Each year hundreds of thousands of visitors come from around the world to view large pueblos such as Wupatki, Elden, and Tuzigoot, in and around the Flagstaff area. They flock to picturesque cliff dwellings at Walnut Canyon, Honanki, Palatki, Montezuma's Castle, and Montezuma's Well. Rock art is commonplace, decorating remote outcrops, mesas, and canyons. Agricultural fields and small field houses—simple shelters used for daily farming chores—appear by the thousands, testifying to the skill and faith of ancient farmers.

For more than a century, the remarkable archaeological remains in the Sierra Sin Agua have attracted scientific and scholarly attention. A great deal is known about the region from oral history and archaeology, but vastly more is still to be learned. The contributors to this book describe recent archaeological studies and offer fresh perspectives on ancient life in the Sierra Sin Agua. Among them are Native American voices speaking about the deeply held meanings of sacred places and ancient sites.

The prehistoric peoples of the Sierra Sin Agua interacted with each other in complex ways at different times, at varying geographical scales—sometimes locally, sometimes across far-reaching distances—and through different forms of social relations. We do not know precisely how they conceived of their group identities or what they called themselves. For that reason, we refer in this book to ancient peoples simply as Hisat'sinom, a Hopi term that translates as "those who lived long ago."

Archaeology in the Sierra Sin Agua returns repeatedly to a few common themes. One is continuity between past and present. The land and its archaeological remains are alive with meaning. Legendary places abound, consisting of points on the landscape that are rugged, large, beautiful, sacred, historically significant, strategically important, well remembered, or any combination of these. Here, people of the past may be gone, but their deeds and contributions to the present live on in the consciousness of the region's Native Americans.

The Flagstaff area holds particular significance for the Hopi people, who maintain religious shrines at local landmarks and continue to make prayers and leave offerings to the Hisat'sinom. In many ways the development of Hopi culture and the archaeology of the Sierra Sin Agua are inseparable. Hopi people know the area just east of the San Francisco Peaks as Pasiwvi, the legendary "place of deliberations." This was where the indigenous Hisat'sinom—descended from the very ancient ones, the Motisinom—and more recent arrivals gathered into pueblo communities and conceived of a new way of living. They rejected the complexity and corruption of older ways in favor of a simpler, humbler, and more difficult life. These principles lie at the core of Hopi cultural values, and they were debated and agreed upon within the walls of places like Elden, Old Caves, and Wupatki Pueblos.

Another theme is the importance of grand geographical features. Two mountains dominate both the landscape and the region's cultural history. First in importance is the San Francisco Peaks. Four distinct summits atop a dormant stratovolcano, the peaks form an eminence massive enough to create its own weather and high enough to be seen from more than 100 miles away. For eight or nine months of the year the peaks are capped with snow. On many days they are covered with clouds, even when the surrounding sky is clear. Summer thunderstorms are born here, coming to life in the early morning as tiny breaths of white clouds at the mountaintop and maturing in the afternoon into dark, booming thunderheads that envelop and drench the surrounding countryside.

At least 14 nearby American Indian groups, including the Yavapais, Havasupais, Hualapais, Navajos, Zunis, Acomas, Mohaves, Hopis, Utes, and Apaches, regard the San Francisco Peaks as a holy place and relate it to their origins and cultural vitality. To the Hopis the peaks are Nuvatukya'ovi, "place of the high snows." To the Navajos they are Dook'o'oos-łííd, "shining on top," a term that also refers to high-elevation snow. In Hopi belief, the Katsinam, spiritual guides and helpers of crucial importance to the world, reside here. Some 700 years ago a Hisat'sinom painter rendered the silhouette of the peaks on the plastered wall of a kiva at Homol'ovi Pueblo, near modern Winslow, Arizona. The painting shows that the peaks were as significant to ancient peoples as they are to modern ones. It would be difficult to overstate the religious, meteorological, and geographical importance of this mountain to the region. The San Francisco Peaks are not just another mountain; they are a transcendent earthly feature and a sacred spiritual home.

Sunset Crater, the other important landform in the area, has an entirely different character. Relative to the San Francisco Peaks, it is a mere bump on the landscape, rising only 1,100 feet above a terrain of cinders and lava. Squat and rounded, this small volcano at first seems indistinguishable from hundreds of similar cinder cones in the surrounding San Francisco volcanic field. But like the peaks, Sunset Crater is vastly more than a physical feature. It is an actor in its own right, a presence whose behavior forever changed the world of ancient local residents. When Sunset Crater finished erupting sometime in the late 1000s CE, it left behind about two billion tons of fresh lava, scoria, and cinders. The eruption was a visually overwhelming, noisy, and no doubt terrifying spectacle that destroyed a large stretch of the landscape, killed wild plants and animals, ruined crops, and drove people from their homes.

It also brought new possibilities. After the eruption, formerly uninhabited areas sprang to life as people adjusted to cinder deposits that, according to some archaeologists, actually brought agricultural success. The cinders acted as a mulch, retaining precious moisture, and they made growing seasons longer by absorbing the sun's heat. Archaeologists traditionally have split the past of the Flagstaff area

Figure 1.2. Aerial view of Sunset Crater, looking southwest.

into "pre-eruption" and "post-eruption" periods, and for good reason. Whether through ecological transformation or coincidence—the debate goes on—the eruption heralded a time of rapid cultural change and florescence.

Another persistent theme is the way early people of the Sierra Sin Agua incorporated and adapted elements of many different cultural traditions into their lives. In the past, as it is today, the Flagstaff area was a geographical and cultural crossroads, a point of contact for people and ideas. Years ago archaeologists tended to put great effort into identifying which of several named "cultures" the people of a given area belonged to. They found it difficult to fit the ancient people around Flagstaff into any one category. In the 1930s and 1940s they vigorously debated whether any of the existing labels, such as Anasazi, Hohokam, and Mogollon—archaeological cultures recognized to the north, south, and southeast of the Flagstaff area, respectively—could accurately be applied to the people of the

Sierra Sin Agua. Some researchers offered new cultural categories such as "Sinagua" and "Cohonina" in an attempt to capture the distinctiveness of local architecture, pottery, and other cultural traits.

Today archaeologists no longer ponder the appropriateness of such classifications, but they still have many questions about the origins of local peoples and the ways in which they moved about, interacted, and changed. What seems clear is that the Hisat'sinom living around the San Francisco Peaks both shared and altered the cultural patterns of their neighbors. They sampled generously from the traditions of others throughout the region, reinventing and recombining cultural elements into unique and eclectic styles that were repeated nowhere else. Only in the Flagstaff area can one admire the architecture of a Chaco Canyon–esque great kiva, perhaps adopted from ancestral Pueblo people in northwestern New Mexico, while standing alongside a Hohokam-style ball court, with its origins in present-day southern Arizona.

Two final and related themes are those of endurance and resilience. From an archaeological perspective, this region has witnessed virtually all the major transitions and developments in the human history of the American Southwest. People began living here as early as at any other place in the Southwest. The most ancient inhabitants date to Paleoindian times, beginning at least 13,100 years ago. When major climatic and environmental changes came at the end of the Pleistocene geological epoch, local people responded in much the same way their counterparts did elsewhere in the Southwest. During the subsequent Archaic period, they changed their technologies and strategies for hunting and food collecting, moving with the seasons to take advantage of the full range of possibilities offered by the Sierra Sin Agua's varied environments. Eventually people adopted agriculture, although it arrived here especially late—not until around 400 CE, or nearly 2,500 years later than in surrounding regions.

After the people became farmers, their populations grew and their cultures changed rapidly. The eruption of Sunset Crater seems to have accelerated these changes. By the mid-1100s, large communities, sophisticated religious systems, far-flung trade relationships, social hierarchies, and territorial boundaries had appeared in the Sierra Sin Agua, paralleling developments in some other corners of the Southwest. In the early 1200s, people began to leave their communities, a process that continued until the century's end. The reasons they left remain elusive, but some combination of worsening climate, exhaustion of natural resources, and social conflicts seems a plausible explanation. Few Native people have lived permanently in the heart of the Sierra Sin Agua since then, although many have traveled through the area over the centuries, sometimes leaving offerings to the memory of Hisat'sinom who once lived here.

Throughout all the changes, a human presence on the general landscape appears to have been continuous—no major gaps exist in the sequence. Native people have endured in this place for more than 130 centuries, surviving and adapting as their world changed around them. The transformations have included climate shifts and major extinctions of large game animals at the end of the Pleistocene; pulses of nearly unbearable heat and drought during the Archaic period; cold spells, droughts, and floods during the farming centuries—not to mention an unexpected volcanic eruption—and an invasion by Europeans and their plants, animals, diseases, technologies, and ideas. Resilience and the ability to adjust with the circumstances were the keys to endurance. The same propensity to adapt in ancient times surely served people well during more recent times of stress. People in and around the Sierra Sin Agua represent true survivors. They have always drawn on the wisdom—and the mistakes—of earlier traditions, remembering and building on older ways to chart new courses forward in the face of environmental and social changes.

In this book we explore these common themes by addressing a wide variety of subjects. Given the vast sweep and complexity of thousands of years of human life in the Sierra Sin Agua, our inherently fragmentary and incomplete stories cannot be tied together into a neat, linear narrative. Instead, we sketch a broad outline of what we currently understand about the ancient past in this place. The following chapters include both anthropological and Native views, often tacking back and forth between scientific knowledge and cultural meaning. This is as it should be. In a place where events of the past are so intimately connected to people of the present, it would be impossible to separate the two.

Christian E. Downum is a professor of anthropology in the Department of Anthropology at Northern Arizona University and former director of the NAU Anthropology Laboratories. He has conducted archaeological research in the Sierra Sin Agua since 1982, mostly at U.S. national parks and monuments. He also serves as archaeological advisor to the Footprints of the Ancestors project, an intergenerational learning program that teaches Native American youths about the ancient places of the American Southwest.

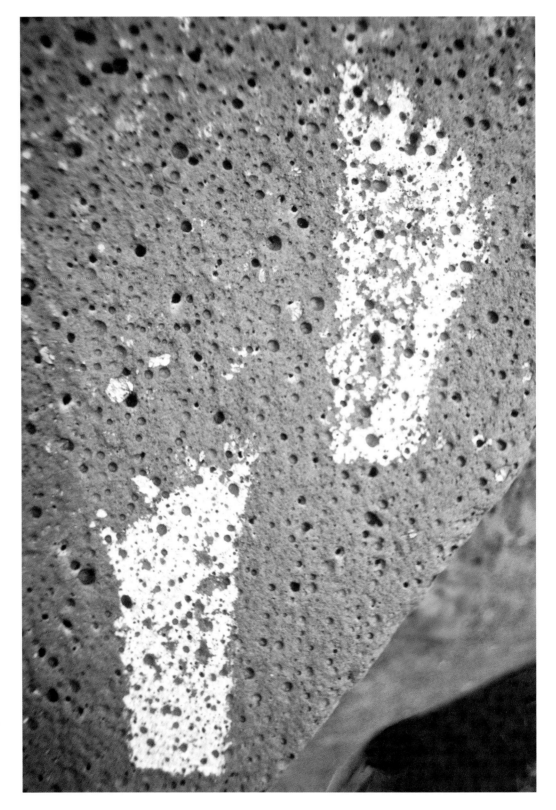

Figure 2.1. Twelfth-century petroglyphs of human footprints on a basalt outcrop near Citadel Ruin, Wupatki National Monument.

Pasiwvi

Place of Deliberations

Leigh J. Kuwanwisiwma, Stewart B. Koyiyumptewa, and Anita Poleahla

Pasiwvi, Hopi for "place of deliberations," refers to the landscape and ancient archaeological sites surrounding modern Flagstaff, Arizona. Pasiwvi represents the cradle of modern Hopi culture, a place where a small group of ancestors developed the major principles of Hopi life, religion, and philosophy. These principles continue to guide Hopi people in the present day.

Pasiwvi is a part of "Hopitutskwa." In the Hopi language, *tutskwa* means "land," so Hopitutskwa means "Hopi land." Hopitutskwa, in concept and in principle, encompasses all land where Hopi ancestors dwelled in the past and where today there exists a spiritual attachment grounded in Hopi religious practice.

In Hopi religion and culture, Hopitutskwa is a compelling concept. It is the area entrusted to the care of Hopi people by Máasaw, the Guardian of the Fourth Era of the human experience. In a covenant with Máasaw, the Hopis agreed to serve as stewards over this land. Thus, contemporary Hopi cultural advisors conceptualize Hopitutskwa as a *homvi'ikya*, a pilgrimage route used to make ritual offerings at a series of shrines, in order to pay homage to a greater domain of stewardship. In this perspective, the area delineated by shrines represents the "plaza," or heartland, with a larger "village" of Hopi ancestral lands lying outside it.

Within Pasiwvi and its immediately surrounding area—the portion of Hopitutskwa shown in figure 2.2—lie dozens of major places and shrines,

a few of which are shown on the map. Each is a profoundly meaningful point on the landscape, and each has a unique name in the Hopi language. These names commemorate thousands of years of human occupation and land use in the area surrounding Nuvatukya'ovi (the San Francisco Peaks). Among them are Öönga (the Hopi salt mines), Potavey'taqa (Point Sublime), and Kooninhahawpi (Havasupai Descent Place), all located in or along the Grand Canyon. Yotse'hahawpi (Apache Descent Place) and Sakwavayu (Clear Creek) sit on the Mogollon Rim. Others are Tokonavi (Navajo Mountain), Tusaqtsomo (Bill Williams Mountain), Hoonawpa (Bear Spring), Tsimontukwi (Woodruff Butte), Namituyqa (Lupton), and Kawestima (Kiet Siel, a pueblo ruin now in Navajo National Monument).

The story of Pasiwvi is retold in Hopi oral traditions. After living on this landscape for a long time, a group of people came together in the place known as Pasiwvi to chart a new course for life. Hopi people hold multiple views about the location of Pasiwvi. Some believe the term refers to a specific, ancient Hopi village. Most believe one archaeological site at the foot of Hovi'itstuykya, Elden Mountain (perhaps Elden Pueblo), was the central location of the Pasiwvi tradition. Others, however, believe that Pasiwvi encompassed the total landscape of Nuvatukya'ovi, within which numerous clan villages were inhabited.

In all versions of the stories about Pasiwvi, important deliberations and decisions happened

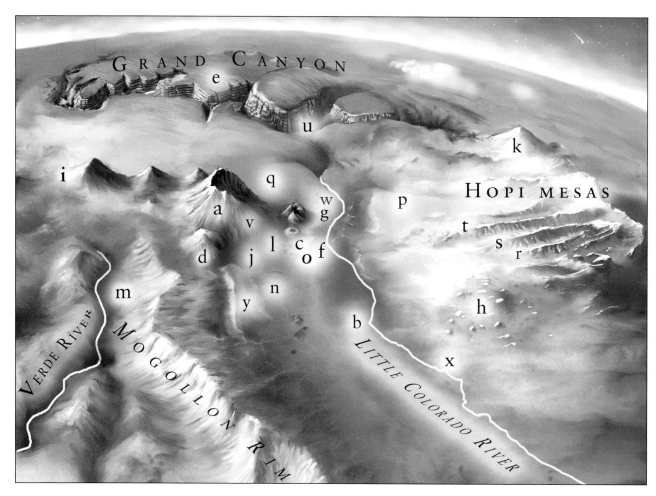

Figure 2.2. Selected Hopi places in and around Pasiwvi, "place of deliberations and acceptance of the covenant (the Hopi way of life)." KEY: *a.* Nuvatukya'ovi (San Francisco Peaks); *b.* Paayu (Palavayu, Little Colorado River); *c.* Palatsmo (Sunset Crater), Patusungwki (ice cave near Sunset Crater), and Yaaptontsa (small cinder cone near Sunset Crater); *d.* Hovi'itstuykya (Elden Mountain); *e.* Öngtupqa (Grand Canyon); *f.* Poosiw (Sootapi, Grand Falls); *g.* Nuva'ovi (Wupatki Pueblo) and Wukoki (Wukoki Pueblo); *h.* Tuutukwi (Hopi Buttes); *i.* Tusaqtsomo (Bill Williams Mountain); *j.* Sawyava or Wupatupqa (Walnut Canyon); *k.* Tokonavi (Navajo Mountain); *l.* Koyongya (Turkey Tanks); *m.* Tsor'ovi (Tuzigoot Pueblo, Tuzigoot National Monument); *n.* Ötöpsikya (Canyon Diablo); *o.* Yuvohayvi or Qa'na'a (Roden Crater, eagle nesting area above Grand Falls); *p.* Munqapi (Moenkopi), Sa'lako (Tuba City); *q.* Tsöötsöptuyi qii'am (home of the antelopes), foothills north of the San Francisco Peaks; *r.* First Mesa; *s.* Second Mesa; *t.* Third Mesa; *u.* Öönga (salt mines in the Grand Canyon); *v.* Pasiwvi (ancient site known to archaeologists as Elden Pueblo); *w.* Hooyapi (crossing place on the Little Colorado River north of Wupatki); *x.* Homol'ovi (ancient Hopi pueblo near Winslow, Arizona); *y.* Nuvakwewtaqa (Chavez Pass).

Traditional histories of the Hopi people usually begin with the people's emergence into this world from the world below. On arrival, they saw the footprints of Máasaw, the caretaker of this earth. He gave the people different languages and lifeways. The Hopi ancestors, in selecting as their life path an ear of short blue corn, chose a life of hardship and humility but one that would be long and fulfilling. So that the people would learn all they needed to know in order to live on the land, Máasaw told them to migrate in all directions, establish villages in which to rest for a while, and then move on until instructed to come together in the center place, now known as the Hopi Mesas. He told them, "Ang kuktota"—"Along there, make footprints." The remains of their houses, broken pottery, stone tools, petroglyphs, burials, and other material remains would be footprints for all who came after them to see and understand.

—*Kelley Hays-Gilpin, based on personal communication from Emory Sekaquaptewa*

within the walls of kivas. During these deliberations, the Motisinom, the original ancient inhabitants of the region, offered a new way known as the Hopi way of life. This new life plan would be distinct from the complex religious ways that had until then held sway. This Hopi life encompassed the principles of Hopi life today: cooperation, sharing, respect, compassion, earth stewardship, and, most of all, humility. Hisat'sinom (a more general term for people from long ago) who came into the area from surrounding regions were welcomed to join in this new philosophy. Eventually, the Hopi philosophy became the guiding principle of modern Hopi clans. "Hopi" therefore refers to a way of life rather than to a specific group of people or a place. The landscape surrounding the San Francisco Peaks reflects the unique history of events leading to the development of Hopi, and the place names the people have given to the land form an integral part of that history.

Leigh J. Kuwanwisiwma, director of the Hopi Cultural Preservation Office, is a member of the Hopi Tribe, the Third Mesa village of Bacavi, and the Greasewood clan. He is a former trustee of the Museum of Northern Arizona and serves on the Tribal Advisory Board of the Arizona State Museum.

Stewart B. Koyiyumptewa, archivist for the Hopi Cultural Preservation Office, is from the Third Mesa village of Hotevilla and is a member of the Badger clan. His interests include historic Hopi photographs and Hopi oratory and oral history.

Anita Poleahla, from Sitsom'ovi, on First Mesa, and a member of the Tansy Mustard clan, is a Hopi language teacher and president of Mesa Media, Inc. She holds master's degrees in education and public administration.

Figure 3.1. Ancient metates—stones used for grinding corn—in a room at Wupatki Pueblo.

They Are Still Here

Wupatki Pueblo and the Meaning of Place

Lyle Balenquah

This chapter is not your standard scientific paper. Unlike most of the other essays in this book, it is nearly devoid of archaeological information, dates, and theories. What follows is simply one person's understanding of what ancient places such as Wupatki Pueblo *mean* to modern Hopi people.

I do not claim to speak for all Hopi people, clans, villages, or religious societies. Each has its own story, and no individual Hopi can claim to know everything about Hopi culture. But I believe a common bond exists among Hopis in the way they think, feel, and know about the homes of their ancestors. This bond is based on a shared understanding of Hopi history that has been handed down across countless generations.

Explaining the meaning of place is no easy task. It requires one to think beyond the hard data of science and Western theoretical frameworks. From a Hopi perspective, the meaning of place is also embedded in the emotional and spiritual realms of human existence—realms that are often disregarded in archaeology because they are not readily testable with scientific methods. Admittedly, it is difficult to measure a person's spiritual or emotional connection to a place. Yet I believe such factors deserve consideration within scientific explanations of the past, especially when those explanations involve Hopi ancestors.

My introduction to Wupatki Pueblo left me wanting to learn more about this place and its inhabitants. As a child, I spent parts of my summer vacations with my family visiting the ancient homes of our ancestors throughout the Four Corners of the American Southwest. We toured many archaeological places, including Mesa Verde, Chaco Canyon, Kiet Siel, and of course Wupatki. I walked amid the preserved remnants of my ancestors' homes and learned that I was a descendant of the people who had built them. I heard stories about the Hisat'sinom, the Ancient People, who possessed remarkable skill, ingenuity, and determination. The stories told of people who could grow crops in the driest of climates, communicate with supernatural forces, and bring rain and snow with the power of their prayers. Yet as a child I did not fully understood what was being said to me. Only later would I come to appreciate the depth and complexity of Hopi ancestry.

Fast forwarding a dozen years, I found myself again among the places of my ancestors. As a student of anthropology at Northern Arizona University, I accepted a part-time job as an archaeological technician with the National Park Service (NPS) in Flagstaff, Arizona. The job reintroduced me to Wupatki Pueblo and the surrounding region.

For the next eight years I studied the science of archaeology and did my best to be an archaeologist. Our main focus at NPS was on documenting the architecture and preserving the ruins at Wupatki and Walnut Canyon National Monuments. Painstakingly we mapped and wrote down descriptions of architectural spaces, features, and materials.

Figure 3.2. Members of the NPS ruins preservation crew at the Wupatki amphitheater, 2002. *Left to right:* Woody Coochwytewa, Mike Cooeyate, Lyle Balenquah, Chris Lowe, Delvin Numkena, Lloyd Masayumptewa, Larsen Harris Jr.

I learned to analyze what I recorded through the lens of scientific inquiry. I filled volumes of data sheets and tables with every conceivable fact about prehistoric building materials and construction styles. I theorized about aspects of social integration and organization. By the end of my sixth year with NPS, I joked with my coworkers—two of whom were also Hopi—that we had probably mapped our millionth wall stone.

Through it all, I wondered who the people were who had built these places of mud and stone. Sometimes while scrutinizing the stone walls of Wupatki, I noticed in the mortar the preserved fingerprints of Hisat'sinom builders. In such moments I recalled the stories I had heard as a child, and in my mind's eye I could see these people as they once were. I often discussed my job with my family at Hopi. They listened intently to my descriptions of architecture and artifacts, and again I heard stories about our ancestors.

This time, though, the details were clearer to me, and more profound. I was now beginning to understand how we Hopi people had come to be who we were. I grasped the way ancestral Hopi clans had traveled far and long across the landscape to the place we now call home. During these travels the people learned how to be Hopi. They learned that being Hopi was not a right but a privilege, hard earned, at great cost of effort. I was also now old enough to participate in certain Hopi ceremonies, and I learned that during those rites, we reenacted our history. I came to understand that our ceremonies and rituals had their origins deep in the ancient past of our ancestors.

I learned from my family members that the artifacts and "ruins" I studied had deeper meanings beyond those my data sheets could reveal. These objects and places were the footprints of our ancestors, and footprints such as Wupatki Pueblo formed physical and spiritual connections to our past. As Leigh Kuwanwisiwma, director of the Hopi Cultural Preservation Office, says, these footprints "are the

Figure 3.3. The Hopi pueblo of Walpi, about 1901.

hallmark of Hopi stewardship" of "ruins, burials, artifacts, shrines, springs, trails, rock writings…and other physical evidence of occupation and use." Archaeological sites, he writes, "are not mere vestiges; Hopi rites and liturgies recognize them as living entities."

The material objects manufactured and built by Hopi ancestors underpin an understanding of our past and help educate present-day Hopi people about both the everyday and the spiritual lives of their ancestors. Through the Hopi teachings I was exposed to, I gained a new lens through which to view the work in which I was participating. That work took on new meaning as I came to better understand my cultural history.

I was fortunate to have entered archaeology at a time when Hopi people were beginning to demand and exercise greater involvement in the work of Southwestern archaeologists, anthropologists, and ethnographers. They expected to be more than simply subjects of scientific inquiry, as they had been in

the past. Through the efforts of tribal departments such as the Hopi Cultural Preservation Office, researchers began placing Hopi interests first in importance when they explored Hopi culture and history. One result of this Hopi-generated research has been the challenging of traditional archaeological concepts and theories about Hopi ancestors. Hopis want to study their ancestors not in the framework of Western science but by using Hopi concepts and knowledge. They seek answers to their own questions about their ancestral past.

One example of the way Hopis choose to achieve this goal has to do with the very definition of their ancestors. Rather than viewing them as neatly defined "cultures" with specific territorial boundaries, Hopi researchers view their ancestors as having been much more dynamic and fluid, with numerous groups or clans making up ancestral populations throughout the Southwest. Classifications such as Sinagua, Anasazi, Cohonina, and Hohokam are peripheral to Hopi research interests. As the

Hopi anthropologist Ferrell Secakuku puts it, simply but confidently, "To Hopi, these are ancestors they call Hisat'sinom, the ancient people."

This designation for the ancestors is always open-ended. Whereas archaeological cultural designations tend to confine groups to certain areas and to the "prehistoric" time period, the Hopi concept of the ancestors implies no such finality. And whereas archaeologists traditionally looked largely at the material objects the ancestors left behind, Hopi understandings of the past enjoy the added dimension of a continual connection to spiritual aspects that are embedded in the material objects.

Much of present-day Hopi culture, including ceremonies and religion, developed during the ancestors' migrations. Over thousands of years they earned and accumulated the knowledge that culminated in the worldview and beliefs expressed through Hopi ceremonies practiced today. This cultural knowledge system, known in Hopi as *wiimi* and *navoti*, is the foundation for the way modern Hopi people remain connected to their ancestral past. Micah Loma'omvaya and T. J. Ferguson explain: "*Navoti* is a historical understanding derived from experiences handed down by ancestors to their descendants. *Wiimi* includes sacred artifacts and the knowledge of how to use them properly in religious ceremonies and rituals. Together, *navoti* and *wiimi* provide both the means to know the past and the ability to invoke the power of the ancestors in the present through ritual offerings and ceremonies."

When a modern Hopi person is involved in ceremonial rites and responsibilities, he or she does not simply go through the motions but actively engages the spiritual power that was first developed and handed down by the ancestors. In this way a Hopi remains connected to the time of the ancestors—many of whom, Hopis believe, still inhabit places such as Wupatki. Indeed, it was in places like these that some Hopi ceremonies, such as the Snake Dance, originated. The ceremonies reflect connections that transcend time and set participants among their ancestors in the present day.

When Hopi people visit such places nowadays, they see not just the remnants of a bygone era but reflections of who they once were and what they have become. They witness the artistic and technical accomplishments of Hopi ancestors and recall their spiritual accomplishments as well. They are reminded that the prosperity of present generations of Hopis depends on the gifts of the departed ancestors. Ferguson and Kuwanwisiwma write, "Ancestral villages that have fallen into ruin are not dead places whose only meaning comes from scientific values. The Hopi ancestors who lived in these villages still spiritually occupy these places." The ancestors play important parts in contemporary Hopi ceremonies that "bring rain, fertility, and other blessings for the Hopi people and their neighbors throughout the world."

The concept that the ancestors remain spiritually alive in ruined villages infuses the Hopi notion that the meaning of the past is what it contributes to life in the present. This understanding provides a continual connection between modern Hopi people and their predecessors. I believe this connection is the bond that Hopi people share in the way they know and feel about their ancestors.

These unique perspectives not only teach Hopis about their cultural history but also help educate others who research and visit ancestral Hopi places. Some Hopi information is included in formal academic efforts to teach archaeologists and anthropologists. In academic research, Hopi knowledge of the past is being incorporated alongside the "hard data" generated through scientific inquiry. The Western scientific process uncovers things such as the material composition and spatial relationships of artifacts—Hopi "footprints"—while Hopi knowledge offers insights into why the artifacts were made and how the ancestors used them. Through archaeological reports, management plans, and other documents, Hopi perspectives on the ancestral past are being disseminated to larger audiences.

Another example of information sharing can be found at the Wupatki Pueblo visitor center, where Hopi perspectives are part of the interpretation of the ruins offered to the visiting public. Exhibits display the values and beliefs Hopi people hold about their ancestors. Through their own words and writings, Hopis' physical and spiritual connections to the homes of their ancestors are expressed in voices only they can provide. These voices show that the

Figure 3.4. Wupatki Pueblo, looking northwest across the Wupatki Basin toward the Doney Cliffs.

builders and inhabitants of places such as Wupatki did not vanish into thin air. They remain in spirit and are ever present in their descendants, who continue to practice the ways the ancestors established thousands of years ago.

During my eight years of work in the Wupatki area, as I interacted almost daily with traces of my Hopi history, I came to know that these monuments of stone and mortar are more than just physical objects on the landscape. They embody the essence of what Hopi culture has come to stand for: cooperation, humility, thoughtful prayer, hard work, and perseverance. These qualities continue to be recognized and honored by modern Hopi people.

Once during my time with NPS, my paternal grandmother and uncle visited me at Wupatki. I accompanied them as they walked the interpretive trail, and I read the trail guide out loud. At certain points my grandmother would interject her own theories and opinions about the remains we looked at. She recalled events from her life's teachings and described the ways certain artifacts were used. She would point to an artifact in front of us and say, "See, this is where we learned how to do such things, and we are still doing it today." Whether my grandmother knew it or not, she was reinforcing the

Hopi sense of place and meaning. The objects in front of us were not just "artifacts," lifeless things that no longer had purpose. Instead, they belonged to someone—they belonged to the Hopis. The place, too, belonged to us, and it was our responsibility to be stewards for its care and protection.

Toward the end of the visit, the three of us split up as each lingered along the trail. Catching up to my grandmother, I heard her voice coming from around the corner of a block of rooms. I could barely make out the words she spoke softly in the Hopi language. At first I thought she was conversing with my uncle, but as I rounded the corner, I saw that she was alone, facing an open room. She smiled when I asked to whom she was talking. Shrugging her shoulders she said, "Nobody, really. But I know that they are still here, listening and watching."

Lyle Balenquah is a member of the Third Mesa Greasewood clan from the village of Paaqavi (Reed Springs). He has worked for more than 10 years as a Hopi archaeologist documenting ancestral Hopi settlements such as Wupatki Pueblo. He holds a master's degree in anthropology from Northern Arizona University in Flagstaff.

Figure 4.1. White painted snake figures at Veit Springs.

Marks on the Land

Rock Art of the Sierra Sin Agua

Kelley Hays-Gilpin and Donald E. Weaver Jr.

Jagged basalt cliffs and boulders rend the green blanket of pine trees enveloping the mountains and mesas of the Sierra Sin Agua. Many of the lava flows were here long before the first humans came to hunt in the forests or farm the rich volcanic soils. These people often marked their trails, shrines, and stopping places with images on stone. Researchers call the images *pictographs* when they are painted on the rock surface and *petroglyphs* when they are incised, pecked, or carved into the rock (plates 8, 9).

Hopi people refer to petroglyphs as *tutuveni*, "footprint marks" left as clan ancestors migrated across the Southwest. For the Hopis, spirals generally signify migration, and certain animal, bird, and geometric figures created near the spirals indicate which clans moved across the landscape. The marks remind knowledgeable viewers of traditional histories and other stories. In their own time, some of the paintings and engravings might have served to mark trails and territorial boundaries. Others might have commemorated visions, successful hunts, migrations, and pilgrimages.

Visitors always want to know, Who made these images? What do they mean? How old are they? We can begin to answer these questions by briefly touring a few of the Sierra Sin Agua's most interesting rock art sites, looking at archaeological clues, and asking how the descendants of ancient peoples, such as the Hopis, interpret the images. Some of the places we describe are open to the public; others cannot be visited until public land managers take

steps to protect them from vandals and inadvertent damage by visitors.

Our journey begins at Veit Springs, nearly 8,500 feet above sea level on the southwestern slopes of the sacred San Francisco Peaks. Veit Springs is special because it includes only painted images—pictographs—which are rare in the region. They survive only where overhangs protect them from rain, ice, and gritty winds.

Just off the paved road that leads toward the summit of the peaks, a well-marked trail winds through aspen groves to Veit Springs. There, red and white painted snakes emerge from a cleft in the rock where water flowed before Euroamerican settlers piped it to a nearby homestead. Perhaps as much as a thousand years ago, people created these snakes by first grinding red pigments, probably hematite, an iron oxide readily available in the region. They mixed the powdered pigment with water and another liquid, perhaps blood, egg, or plant juice, to make paint. They drew the long zigzag shapes with their fingers or with brushes made of fibrous yucca leaves.

For many indigenous peoples across the Americas, the motion of snakes evokes both moving water and lightning. Interpreting rock art is often difficult, but in the case of Veit Springs, painting snakes next to a spring high on a mountain where summer thunderstorms build seems easy to understand.

Far more common than paintings on rock in the Sierra Sin Agua are petroglyphs, or rock engravings.

Figure 4.2. Water bird and geometric figures at Picture Canyon.

Look for them on basalt outcrops, especially on cliff faces and boulders along drainages. People made most of these images by pecking the naturally weathered rock surface with a cobble, revealing fresh rock below. The contrast between darker, weathered surfaces and lighter-colored underlying rock makes the shallow engravings visible. Over time, as the freshly exposed surface weathers to a darker color, pecked images fade from view. When younger, lighter figures appear alongside older, darker rock carvings—especially when younger images are superimposed on older ones—researchers can build relative chronologies of petroglyph styles.

Another way of situating petroglyphs in time is to compare them with designs found on painted pottery, because pottery styles have often been tied to tree-ring dates (see chapter 6). The three petroglyph sites we describe next seem to date mostly between about 1100 and 1400 CE, a judgment based on image style, cross-dating with pottery, and the associations of the sites with places where we know people lived at certain times.

Our first site is on the Rio de Flag, which descends from the southwestern slopes of the San Francisco Peaks and runs eastward past Elden Pueblo. The river once flowed freely into a narrow canyon where ancient hunters, farmers, and travelers depicted long-legged water birds, game animals, and other figures on the basalt cliffs and boulders. Today this place is called Picture Canyon because it boasts one of the largest concentrations of Hisat'sinom rock art in the Sierra Sin Agua.

Seven rock art clusters can be found in and along the edges of this small but spectacular, basalt-walled box canyon. Nearby lie several buried pit houses, the remains of stone buildings, large surface scatters of pottery and other artifacts, and room-size rings of rock that probably mark where farmhouses once stood. Clearly, Hisat'sinom lived here—sometimes large numbers of them.

Petroglyphs typical of the "Sinagua culture," a name archaeologists apply to the ancient farming people of this area, dominate the 126 rock art panels and more than 735 individual elements at Picture Canyon. Human and humanlike figures (anthropomorphs) and animals (zoomorphs) predominate among the images of living creatures. The petroglyph makers depicted water birds, bird tracks, snakes, insects, lizards, horned toads, and pawprints. They captured the human form in various poses, sometimes as simple stick figures and sometimes as full-bodied persons. Archers stand frozen in the act of carrying or drawing their bows.

Here and there, images of human footprints, including a cluster of baby-size prints, march across the rock. Four-legged creatures appear in profile, in too little detail for us to identify species. They could be dogs, deer, elk, bighorn sheep, or other animals. A few, however, show branched antlers that could belong only to a deer or an elk.

Occasionally an unknown artist engraved an entire scene. Three scenes show hunts in progress, with an archer nearing his quarry. Another features a row of four identical, four-legged animals climbing vertically up a panel. A third portrays two large people and three smaller ones—perhaps a long-ago family portrait.

Abstract, or geometric, designs are also common at Picture Canyon. Viewers can discern spirals, circles, concentric circles, rayed circles, rayed concentric circles (often described as sun symbols), zigzags, wavy lines, crosses, outlined crosses, and complex geometric shapes.

Many of the images seen at Picture Canyon are ubiquitous across the prehistoric Southwestern landscape, but a few appear to be diagnostic of Sinagua rock art. Among the quintessentially Sinagua petroglyphs are anthropomorphs with prominent, round bellies, as well as complex geometric designs resembling those found on pottery and textiles.

The Hopi, Navajo, and Yavapai tribes identify Picture Canyon as a traditional cultural place used by their ancestors and still spiritually important today. Preserving the site, though, is becoming ever more challenging. A wastewater treatment plant lies upstream, and hiking trails, pipelines, roads, and

fences crisscross the area. Vandals have looted nearby pit houses and caves, defaced the rock surfaces with names and dates, and dumped trash over the cliffs. Many Flagstaff citizens and state, city, and county government officials hope to work with the tribes to restore this landscape and protect the petroglyphs and other ancient remains.

Approximately 35 miles southeast of the San Francisco Mountains, the northern edge of tree-covered Anderson Mesa forms a high basalt escarpment overlooking grasslands south of the Little Colorado River valley. Hundreds of petroglyphs mark the boulders of Anderson Pass (plate 10). Twenty-three rock art sites, most small clusters of fewer than 20 panels, have been recorded in the area. We know people lived near these sites because archaeologists have found the remains of several pit-house villages, a large stone masonry structure (known as Anderson Fort), room-size rock rings, and many scatters of surface artifacts.

The rock art at Anderson Pass features large numbers of geometric forms including meandering lines, zigzags, crosses, circles, spirals, and grids. Stick figures and full-bodied beings, some with exaggerated hands or feet, round midsections, and male genitalia, strike poses on the dark basalt boulders and outcrops. Among the animals, some with horns seem to be bighorn sheep, and those with long, curving tails look like mountain lions. We also find birds with outstretched wings, lizards, insectlike forms (probably dragonflies), human footprints and handprints, pawprints, and bird tracks. Scenes made up of multiple petroglyphs are rare, but artisans sometimes created paired images such as twin footprints or side-by-side animals.

Depictions of footprints suggest that important trails once cut through Anderson Pass, making it a crossroads as well as a busy neighborhood. Hopi migration traditions indicate that many clans traveled among these places on their way to their pre-destined center place on the Hopi Mesas.

One set of figures stands out from the usual Sinagua-style petroglyphs at Anderson Pass. On a single panel, seven anthropomorphs with elaborate headdresses and raised arms stand on flat, elongated objects. One rock art researcher, drawing on his

anthropomorph　　foot print　　hand print　　hunter

lizard　　Kakaka　　mountain lion　　waterbird

plant-like figure　　insect-like figure　　complex abstract life form　　spreadwing bird

bighorn sheep　　game trap　　bird tracks　　complex geometric form

concentric circles　　spiral　　squared spiral　　interlocking connected square spirals

squiggle　　tailed circle / oval / disc　　cross　　outlined cross　　rayed circle　　grid

Figure 4.3. Some common petroglyph types of the Sierra Sin Agua.

Figure 4.4. A lizard or humanlike figure with a round belly, at Picture Canyon. This kind of figure is characteristic of rock art of the Sinagua archaeological culture.

own cultural experiences, thought these objects looked like surfboards, so some people now know this place by the whimsical name "Surfer." From a more appropriate cultural perspective, these beings closely resemble depictions of Yavapai supernaturals known as Kakaka, who are associated with lightning. Anderson Pass lies north of the historic Yavapai homeland in the Verde Valley, and the figures might mark a territorial boundary or trails used for trade between Yavapai ancestors and Hopi villagers to the north.

The last stop on our rock art tour is Chavez Pass, or Nuvakwewtaqa, meaning "wearing a snow belt"—a

Figure 4.5. Geometric and animal figures on a boulder at Anderson Pass.

Figure 4.6. Kakaka figures at Anderson Pass.

Hopi term referring to a white strip of snow along the north slopes of Anderson Mesa. Chavez Pass holds 33 recorded rock art sites, mostly small clusters of fewer than 15 panels, all within just over a mile of three large, hilltop pueblos where Hisat'sinom lived between the late 1200s and the early 1400s. The remains of some pit houses, isolated blocks of rooms, farming terraces, and a reservoir or ball court also appear in the vicinity. Centuries ago, bustling communities stood here.

Artists made their marks in basalt boulder fields and on low cliff faces bordering the flat summit of Anderson Mesa, the major topographic feature north-northwest of Chavez Pass. The pass formed part of a strategically important and well-documented travel route connecting the Hopi Mesas with the Verde Valley. Hopi traditions identify Chavez Pass as an important migration "staging area," where

clans stayed for a generation or two before traveling on to the Homol'ovi pueblos near Winslow and then to their final destination, today's Hopi villages.

Geometric forms predominate among the Chavez Pass images, but a few humanlike figures cling to the rock, some with round midsections and exaggerated hands, feet, fingers, and toes. Archers clutch bows as they stalk and shoot their quarry. Human hand- and footprints, bird tracks, quail, deer or elk, desert bighorn sheep, dogs, pawprints, snakes, insectlike forms, and plantlike forms all appear here and there.

Chavez Pass also features a rare type of petroglyph that we originally called "rabbit ears" for its resemblance to old, indoor television antennas. In fact the image depicts a prehistoric game trap, a V-shaped construction of stone or brush that funneled

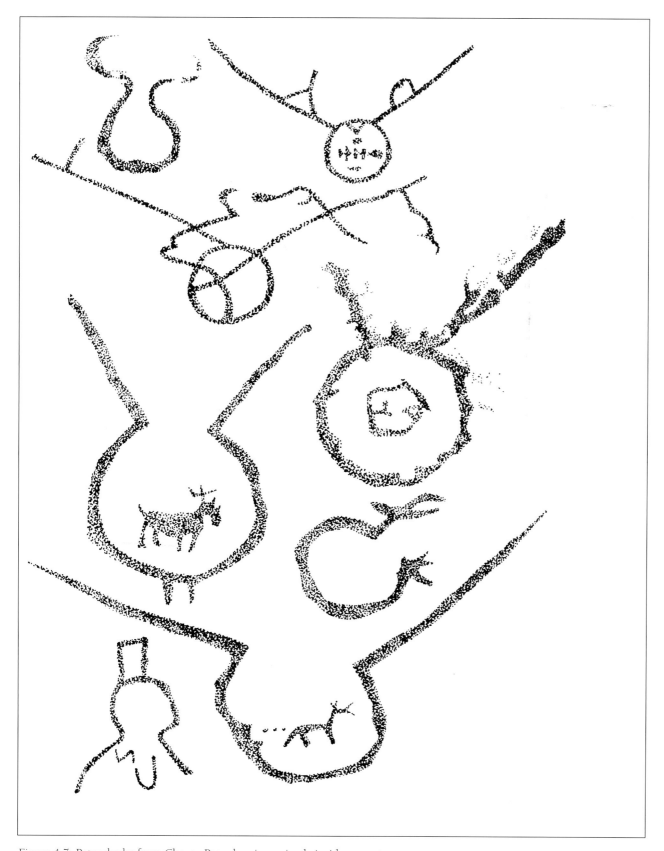

Figure 4.7. Petroglyphs from Chavez Pass showing animals inside game traps.

Figure 4.8. Abstract life forms apparently unique to Chavez and Anderson Passes. Note the circular midsections on the examples at center foreground and far right. Two others appear in the right background.

animals into a circular killing zone where hunters lay in wait. Several petroglyphs in this district clearly show animals entering or already inside a trap.

Researchers do not know quite what to make of one of the most unusual images, a large, humanlike form with too many arms or legs, a round midsection, and an elaborate headdress. This unusual creature seems to be unique to the rock art of Chavez and Anderson Passes.

Paradoxically, rock art is among the most durable of ancient cultural remains yet one of the most vulnerable and easily damaged in the modern world. What natural weathering has not destroyed over thousands of years can be scarred or obliterated in minutes by careless visitors, modern construction, recreational vehicles, or vandals with chisels or spray paint. Even people who love to study rock art can be a threat. In the past, researchers harmed images by applying chalk to them so that

they would show up better in photographs and by making rubbings of them on paper. We believe the preservation of rock art depends on community-based education and stewardship. Anyone can learn to record rock art responsibly, serve as a site steward —someone who watches a petroglyph site and reports vandalism to the proper authorities—or teach others to behave respectfully in such places. Working together, we can all help ensure that these remarkable messages from the past endure for the future.

Kelley Hays-Gilpin, a professor of anthropology at Northern Arizona University and curator of anthropology at the Museum of Northern Arizona, has studied rock art and pottery in the Southwest for nearly 30 years. Among her many published books and articles, her *Ambiguous Images: Gender and Rock Art* won the 1995 Society for American Archaeology book award.

Donald E. Weaver Jr. served as head of the Department of Anthropology at the Museum of Northern Arizona before forming a private consulting company, Plateau Mountain Desert Research. He has investigated rock art in Arizona for more than 30 years and served as president of the American Rock Art Research Association, the major organization supporting such research in the United States.

For information on becoming a site steward, please visit the Arizona State Parks website at www.pr.state.az.us/partnerships/shpo/sitestew.html. Many other states have similar programs. To learn about taking part in rock art research, visit the American Rock Art Research Association's website at www.arara.org.

Figure 5.1. Aerial view of Sunset Crater (upper left), looking south.

Fire in the Sky

The Eruption of Sunset Crater Volcano

Mark D. Elson and Michael H. Ort

No one who watched the eruption of Sunset Crater in the late eleventh century likely ever forgot its seemingly supernatural power. Molten rock spewed from deep within the earth, covering the landscape with thick layers of ash and cinders. The ground rumbled and shook for miles around. Perhaps as many as 2,000 farmers from surrounding villages became "volcano refugees." More than 900 years later, the Hopis and other tribes in the area still remember the volcano's outburst in their oral traditions.

Sunset Crater rises just east of the San Francisco Peaks, about nine miles north of Flagstaff, Arizona. It is one of some 600 volcanic features dating from about 6 million to only about 900 years ago in the 1,800-square-mile San Francisco volcanic field. This expanse of volcanoes, lava flows, and cinder deposits, or "black sand," rises high above the surrounding Colorado Plateau and helps give the Sierra Sin Agua its unique geological and environmental character.

The Sunset Crater eruption was not, in fact, a single, discrete event. The crater is only the largest volcanic feature along an eruption fissure—a crack in Earth's crust that allows magma, or molten rock, to rise to the surface—running about six miles from southeast to northwest. Many other volcanic features also arose during the relatively rapid series of events generally referred to as the Sunset Crater eruption. For example, southeast of Sunset Crater lie small piles of cinders and lava known as Vent 512 and Gyp Crater, which formed early in the

eruption sequence. At least six other small cinder cones formed along the fissure, along with spatter cones (formed by splashes of lava), fumaroles (openings that emit steam and gas), and a nearly three-mile-long, thin lava flow fed from a low spatter cone.

Two major lava flows—the Bonito flow and the Kana'a flow—issued from the base of Sunset Crater and hardened into jagged expanses of rock. Eventually the lava flowing from these two primary vents covered about three square miles under 5 to 100 feet of dark gray rock. Cinders and ash blanketed hundreds of square miles to depths ranging from about an inch north of Wupatki National Monument to hundreds of feet at the crater itself. When Sunset Crater finally quieted, about two billion tons of new ash, cinders, and lava lay on the ground.

Despite this fiery drama, cinder cones like Sunset Crater are relatively low-key volcanoes. They do not resemble the large, towering stratovolcanoes of popular imagination, such as Mount Fuji in Japan, Krakatau in Indonesia, and Mount St. Helens in Washington. Stratovolcanoes—including the San Francisco Peaks—can build to thousands of feet through intermittent, often violent eruptions over hundreds of thousands of years. Cinder cones are smaller, produce smaller explosions, and typically form over weeks to months.

A cinder-cone eruption typically begins when sheets of lava shoot from a volcanic fissure, forming a "curtain of fire." Eventually, what began as a linear

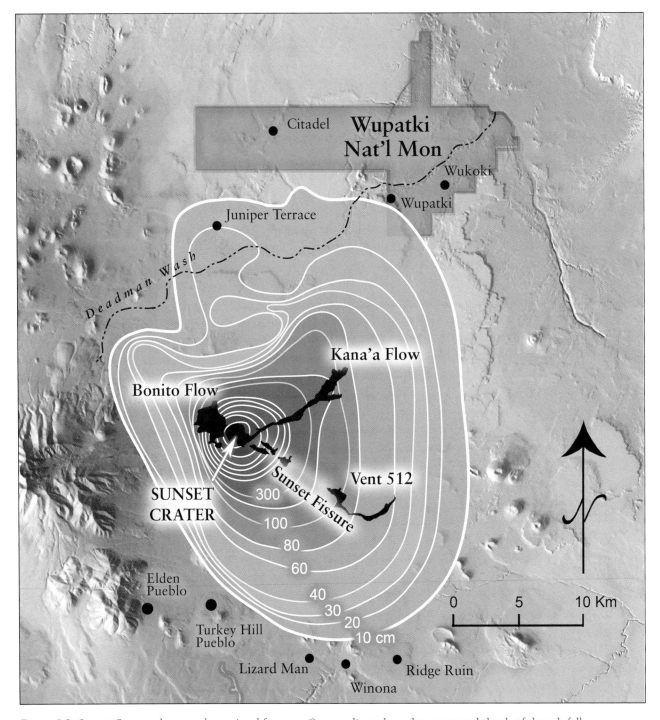

Figure 5.2. Sunset Crater volcano and associated features. Contour lines show the extent and depth of the ash fall.

breach in Earth's crust closes to form one or a few conduits for the upwelling magma (which, when it reaches Earth's surface, is called lava). The ongoing eruption continues from these vents, building a main cinder cone. "Fountaining" throws molten lava ("spatter") and cinders hundreds to thousands of feet into the air. The cinders are silt- to cobble-

size particles of hardened lava shot through with air bubbles. As the eruption of a cinder cone proceeds, lava oozes from vents near its base. This lava moves slowly enough that people can often outwalk or outrun it. It destroys property but rarely causes injuries or deaths.

Well-documented eruptions of cinder cones are

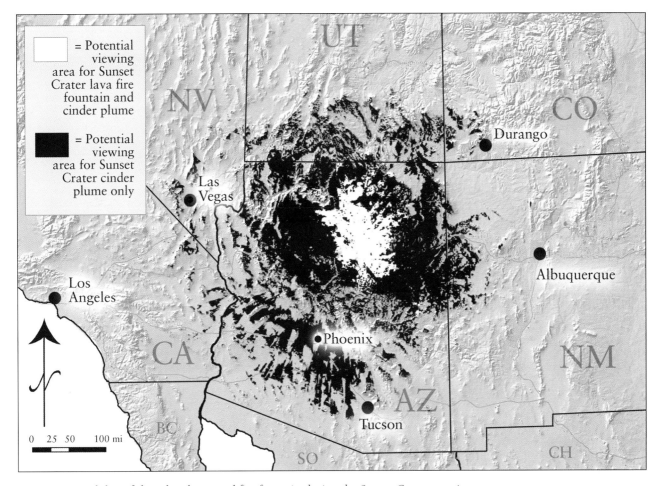

Figure 5.3. Visibility of the ash column and fire fountain during the Sunset Crater eruption.

rare, but one important example is Paricutín, a 1,400-foot-high volcano that erupted between 1943 and 1952 in Michoacán, Mexico. Paricutín is often considered a "twin" of Sunset Crater because of its similarity in size, eruption sequence, and surrounding environment. Both volcanoes erupted in forested highlands cultivated by corn farmers.

Judging from the behavior of Paricutín, which is well known from eyewitness accounts and scientific investigations, ominous signs likely foreshadowed the emergence of Sunset Crater. Earthquakes might have rumbled for weeks or months before the eruption. At Paricutín, the first noticeable sign was an earthquake that struck 45 days before the volcano began to form. A week later, the ground began to shake daily. In the week before the volcano formed, earthquakes hit at the rate of 25 to 30 a day. Finally, on the day before the eruption, 300 earth tremors were recorded.

Cinder cones can grow amazingly fast. At Paricutín, the cinder cone grew out of a 4-foot-deep hole in a cornfield to tower some 550 feet in a mere six days. By the end of its first year, it had reached 1,100 feet, or 80 percent of its final height. In a similar time frame, the Sunset Crater volcano reached a height of almost 900 feet above the surrounding countryside, with a base encompassing around 500 acres. When the eruption ended, the volcano was about 1,100 feet tall.

Clouds of cinders and steam during a volcanic eruption create their own weather system, producing thunder and lightning. The heavy ash and cinder fall from Sunset Crater, along with smoke from accompanying forest fires, must have darkened the daytime sky. At night the horizon glowed a fiery red. People hundreds of miles away would have been able to hear the roar of the eruption, a noise comparable to heavy surf or continuous artillery

Figure 5.4. Cinder-filled pit house about two miles west of Sunset Crater, excavated by the Museum of Northern Arizona in the early 1930s. People built this pit house around 835 CE and lived in it for several years. About two centuries later its remains were filled with thick layers of volcanic cinders ejected by Sunset Crater.

fire. For people who had previously never heard anything louder than a clap of thunder, this barrage of sound surely was frightening and awe inspiring.

Volcanologists estimate that the Sunset Crater cinder plume rose two to three miles high and would have been visible on a clear day for up to 250 miles—far enough to be seen by people then living in or near Chaco Canyon, the Phoenix Basin, and the Four Corners area. The crater's lava fire fountain, reaching 850 to 2,200 feet high, was another spectacular sight, especially at night. It was visible across a smaller area than the ash plume but still could have been seen from 150 miles away in southern Utah and across much of central Arizona. Even more people might have noticed the glow of the fire fountain reflected by distant clouds. Clearly,

most residents of the greater Southwest at the time must have been well aware that something unusual was happening in the Sierra Sin Agua.

The affected area was not uninhabited wilderness. In the summer of 1930, archaeologists from the Museum of Northern Arizona uncovered an ancient pit house sealed beneath a thick layer of black cinders. Their discovery offered the first proof that Sunset Crater had erupted at a time when Hisat'sinom were living in northern Arizona, and not thousands of years earlier.

Indeed, until recently archaeologists and geologists thought the eruption began in precisely the year 1064 CE. The dendrochronologist Terah Smiley proposed that date in the late 1950s after he observed a pattern of thin rings in a few tree specimens from

Wupatki Pueblo. He believed the thin rings showed the effects of the Sunset Crater eruption, and the pattern started in late 1064. Dendrochronologists now understand that environmental factors unrelated to volcanic eruptions can produce ring-width patterns identical to those Smiley observed. Still, comparisons of well-dated archaeological structures that do and do not contain Sunset Crater cinders show that the initial eruption took place sometime between 1050 and 1100. Recent analyses of the chemistry of tree rings in beams found in structures within the cinder blanket show that in the mid-1080s, the trees experienced increased availability of chemicals that are concentrated in fresh volcanic material. This may correspond to the eruption date.

How long did the eruption last? About 95 percent of historically known cinder cones have completed their eruptions in less than a year, and 50 percent in less than a month. Paricutín's nine years of eruptions are among the longest on record. To find out how long Sunset Crater stayed active, we carried out paleomagnetic dating of its lava flows, building on earlier research by Duane Champion and Eugene Shoemaker of the U.S. Geological Survey.

Paleomagnetic dating relies on measurements of the orientation of magnetic particles in basalt lava. When molten lava cools and solidifies, its magnetic field becomes forever aligned with the position of Earth's magnetic pole at the time of cooling. The magnetic pole wanders over time, and scientists have plotted its position as it moved. Therefore, they can compare the orientation of the magnetic field in lava with the map of Earth's magnetic poles to estimate when the lava cooled.

Our study revealed that Sunset Crater was active for no more than 50 years and perhaps as briefly as a few weeks or months. Supporting this finding, excavations of cinder deposits show that none of the eight discrete layers of cinders laid down during the eruptions was much eroded, nor did much windblown sand lie between the layers. In other words, wind and water had little time to weather away or bury one layer before another fell on top of it.

We also calculated the length of time it took for the Kana'a lava flow to reach its greatest extent. We began by figuring the minimum speed needed for lava of this type, flowing across the landscape without cooling and hardening, to reach its maximum distance. Dividing the total volume of the Kana'a flow by that discharge rate, we estimated that the flow lasted only 23 to 115 days. The Bonito flow did not lend itself to such calculations, but the two flows probably ended within days to weeks of each other. Both have sectors with no cinders on them, indicating that they postdate the end of cinder deposition.

The lava flows and cinder fall from Sunset Crater must have disrupted people's lives enormously. Lava probably destroyed many Hisat'sinom houses and fields. Fires sparked by the eruption must also have forced people to flee their homes, at least temporarily. All plants within about five miles of the volcano, including crops, were killed. Cinder fall could have damaged even areas far removed from the volcano. Data from modern eruptions show that only four to six inches of cinders are enough to collapse modern roofs. Prehistoric houses as far away as Wupatki National Monument might have sustained damage.

At Paricutín, an estimated 5,000 cattle and horses died from breathing the fine ash emitted early in the eruption. At Sunset Crater, it is likely that the cinder fall, smoke from lava-ignited forest fires, and volcanic gases sickened many people, particularly the very young and the elderly. Those who experienced the eruption at close range might have had lifelong respiratory problems and died early as a result.

Ultimately, in addition to its detrimental effects, the Sunset Crater eruption produced some benefits for humans. At the end of the eleventh century, just after the eruption, the density of settlements in the area increased dramatically. To explain this sudden surge in population, the scientist Harold S. Colton proposed that thin layers of newly deposited Sunset Crater cinders acted as a water-retaining mulch, enabling people to farm in previously unproductive areas. Colton thought the opening of new land for settlement encouraged people to migrate into the Flagstaff area—a "prehistoric land rush," he called it. Interaction between the newcomers and the remaining local people changed the lives of both. More recent researchers, such as Christian Downum and Alan Sullivan, have adopted Colton's theory to argue that the cinder mulch was

Figure 5.5. Hardened lava and cinders in the Sunset Crater volcanic landscape.

People who moved into the newly productive corn-growing areas had to develop an agricultural technology geared toward "cinder management." Keeping a consistent, one- to three-inch layer of cinders over their fields was no easy task in a place buffeted by strong seasonal winds. Throughout this area, especially in the vicinity of Wupatki National Monument, archaeologists find many stone alignments oriented perpendicular to the prevailing wind direction (rather than perpendicular to slope). These alignments served as windbreaks and probably trapped cinders (see chapter 16).

The volcano buried hundreds of farmsteads and thousands of acres of arable land, but the Hisat'sinom who coped with the Sunset Crater eruption apparently thrived. At least some of the volcano refugees eventually built the villages whose ruins now dot the landscape in and around Wupatki National Monument. The small scale of their relatively egalitarian, subsistence-level society allowed them to respond rapidly to the damage caused by the eruption. With villages widely dispersed, the people worst affected by the eruption were probably able to move in with kin in more sheltered areas. Agricultural fields, too, were small and widely scattered, so farming could be restarted quickly. The Sunset Crater eruption was a relatively small one, leaving places within 6 to 12 miles of the cinder cone undamaged and available for resettlement. The rain of cinders over the Wupatki area opened up new, uninhabited, and possibly unclaimed land for settlement.

For current residents of Flagstaff and north-central Arizona, the question is not *whether* another eruption will occur in the San Francisco volcanic field but *when*. Besides Sunset Crater, two other eruptions took place in the volcanic field within the past 20,000 years. At least one of these, the eruption of SP Crater, was probably also witnessed by prehistoric eyes. The next eruption probably won't happen in our lifetime, but it undoubtedly

an important factor in the initial settlement and subsequent population growth at Wupatki National Monument (see chapter 11).

Recent corn-growing experiments by botanist Gwendolyn Waring strongly support Colton's theory. At an experimental plot she planted near Wupatki, corn germinated only when covered by one to three inches of cinders, and not when planted in uncovered soil. Conversely, too much cinder cover—six inches or more—greatly reduced the rate of corn germination.

To help understand which areas might have been most productive for ancient farmers, we measured the depth of undisturbed Sunset Crater cinders in various places around the Sierra Sin Agua and created a map showing the thicknesses of the deposits (fig. 5.2). We found that the eruption covered an area of about 150 square miles with more than 12 inches of cinders. On the basis of Waring's experiment, we concluded that farming was impossible in this area until wind and water erosion had reduced the cinder cover by at least half. Farther away—at lower elevations—the devastating event covered the ground with only one to three inches of cinders. This cinder mulch increased water retention and, together with the longer growing seasons characteristic of lower elevations, made many places suddenly much more desirable for farming.

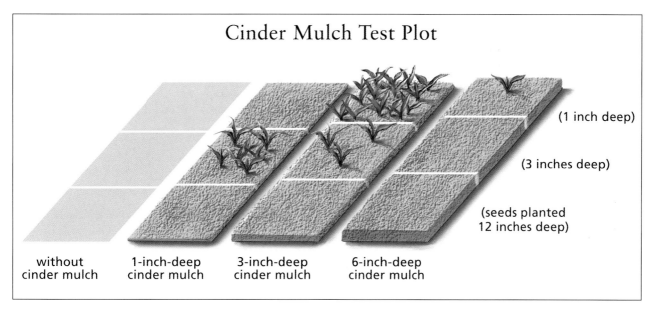

Figure 5.6. Results of corn growth experiments in volcanic cinders. At a moderate depth, cinders provide a mulching effect that helps corn germinate and grow.

will awe some generation of our descendants. Future researchers will get to see whether the response to the next volcano is as efficient and successful as that of the Hisat'sinom.

Mark D. Elson is a research archaeologist and principal investigator at Desert Archaeology, Inc.

Michael H. Ort is a volcanologist and a professor in the School of Earth Sciences and Environmental Sustainability at Northern Arizona University. For the past 15 years, the two have collaborated on deciphering the Sunset Crater eruption and the resulting human adaptations to this catastrophic event.

Figure 6.1. A. E. Douglass coring a ponderosa pine tree to extract a sample of its tree rings, Forestdale Valley, Arizona, 1928.

Trees, Time, and Environment

Jeffrey S. Dean

Dendrochronology—the use of tree rings to date past human and natural events and to reconstruct past environments—is probably the only science ever invented in the Southwest. Like many other sciences, it arose almost by accident, inspired by a mundane wagon ride. Unlike many other sciences, it was the idea of a single person, the extraordinary polymath Andrew Ellicott Douglass. Today Douglass's science helps archaeologists understand everything from the year and season in which a prehistoric pueblo was built to the lengths and strengths of prehistoric droughts and cold spells.

In 1901, Flagstaff, Arizona, was a small mercantile, lumbering, and railroad town. That year, a buckboard wagon carried A. E. Douglass, an astronomer, from Flagstaff to the Grand Canyon and back. Born in Windsor, Vermont, in 1867, Douglass had come to Flagstaff in 1894 to help construct and run an observatory for the Boston astronomer Percival Lowell. Besides working at the Lowell Observatory, he taught at what is now Northern Arizona University. In 1906 he joined the University of Arizona, where, over the next 55 years, he taught physics, astronomy, geography, and dendrochronology. He also founded and directed both the university's Steward Observatory and its Laboratory of Tree-Ring Research (LTRR).

In Flagstaff Douglass studied the effects of sunspots on the earth's climate. Frustratingly, he was unable to establish a relationship between annual rainfall and the 22-year sunspot cycle,

because no local weather records were long enough to reveal comparable cycles of precipitation. That day in 1901, jolting across a landscape timbered with ponderosa pines, he was struck by the difference between the semiarid Arizona forest and the humid woods of his native New England. The latter were dense and choked with brush; the former featured widely spaced trees and a sparse undergrowth of grasses and pine seedlings. Because scientists then believed that competition among plants regulated the annual growth of rings in Northeastern trees, Douglass wondered whether the dry environment, wide spacing of trees, and scant underbrush might mean that Arizona tree-ring growth was controlled by precipitation. If so, then the ring widths of Flagstaff-area pines might contain the long rainfall records Douglass needed.

Examining ponderosa pine logs, Douglass found that sequential variations in ring widths matched from tree to tree. By correlating identical patterns of ring widths among trees from a large area—a technique known as *crossdating*—he could assign individual rings in different trees to the same growth year. When the calendar date of one ring in the sequence was known, he could assign calendar dates to all the rings in the series.

The observation that trees crossdated with each other over great distances pointed to a large-scale causal factor that could only be climate. Indeed, Douglass discovered that ring width corresponded to the precipitation of the preceding winter: wet winters produced wide rings in subsequent years, and dry winters produced narrow rings. Crossdating four centuries of ring patterns common to all trees in the Flagstaff area, the astronomer now had a chronology recording annual precipitation back into the 1400s—long enough by far to support his sunspot studies. Circumstances, however, diverted his research in an unexpected direction: archaeology.

The anthropologist Clark Wissler, of the American Museum of Natural History in New York City, learned of Douglass's work and wondered whether tree rings could be used to date wooden beams preserved in ruins in northwestern New Mexico. Wissler sent Douglass wood samples for crossdating. The results showed that construction at Pueblo Bonito, in Chaco Canyon, preceded that at nearby Aztec Ruins by 50 years. For the first time in American archaeology, prehistoric events had been related to each other in terms of absolute years. But Wissler's samples failed to crossdate with the Flagstaff chronology, so the actual calendar dates of the New Mexico sites remained unknown.

The demonstration that dendrochronology had archaeological potential launched an effort to construct a tree-ring chronology long enough to allow the absolute dating of Wissler's samples and others. In 1929 a charred wood fragment from Whipple Ruin, at Show Low, Arizona, linked the dated Flagstaff chronology with an undated, 585-year "floating" chronology based on samples from many Southwestern prehistoric sites. To the delight of archaeologists, Douglass announced calendar dates, accurate to the year, for scores of sites, among them Whipple and Pinedale Ruins in east-central Arizona, Pueblo Bonito and Aztec in northwestern New Mexico, Cliff Palace and Spruce Tree House on Mesa Verde in southwestern Colorado, and Betatakin, Kiet Siel, Wupatki, and the Citadel in northern Arizona. After 1929 Douglass curtailed his archaeological

Figure 6.2. Ponderosa pine trees growing in deep cinder deposits near Sunset Crater. These trees form annual growth rings that reflect year-to-year variation in local precipitation.

work, but others made it an integral component of the LTRR's continuing mission. At present, more than 50,000 dates have been derived from more than 5,000 Southwestern archaeological sites.

Far from working in isolation, Douglass received aid, encouragement, and collaboration from other people and institutions in Flagstaff. Harold S. Colton (see fig. 10.4), founder of the Museum of Northern Arizona (MNA), was a close friend as well as an archaeological mentor and consultant to Douglass. He guided the astronomer to suitable wood sources and helped select Whipple Ruin as a place to search for the link between the dated and undated chronology segments. Lyndon L. Hargrave (see fig. 10.3), field director at MNA, led many of the expeditions that collected the samples used to build the ring chronology. Advantageously situated in the middle of the pine forest, MNA became the de facto headquarters of the chronology-building project. It was the setting in which archaeologist Emil W. Haury (see fig. 10.2) conducted a "blind" duplication of Douglass's analysis, which independently verified the crossdating and the master chronology. This confirmation of the validity of dendrochronology helped Southwestern archaeologists to accept it rapidly.

Once Douglass and his colleagues had established the master ring chronology, they turned their

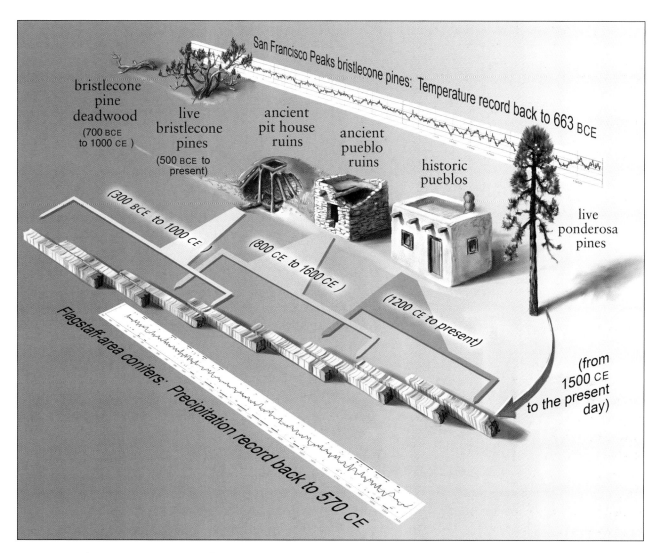

Figure 6.3. Schematic representation of crossdating, showing major principles and sources of materials used to produce a local tree-ring chronology, along with graphs of climatic reconstructions based on tree-ring samples from the Flagstaff area.

attention to dating sites and archaeological sequences in different places. Although Douglass remained the arbiter of tree-ring practices and results, other institutions, including MNA, created their own tree-ring programs to expedite work on local chronological issues. Hargrave scoured the landscape for archaeological sites that might contribute to a chronology for the ancient peoples of the San Francisco volcanic field. If test excavations failed to yield tree-ring samples in the form of charcoal, Hargrave closed the dig and moved on to a new site.

The tree-ring samples quickly amassed through this procedure went to MNA staff dendrochronologist John C. McGregor (see fig. 10.2) for immediate analysis and then to Douglass for checking. Within

a decade, firm dates were assigned to the periods in Colton's chronological schemes for the Sinagua and other archaeologically defined cultures of the area. Subsequent work has refined these chronologies, but the basic outlines established in the 1930s remain solid. Archaeological excavations in the 1930s also revealed that the eruption of the Sunset Crater volcano had disrupted people's lives in the area late in the eleventh century (see chapter 5).

Another accomplishment was the accurate dating of ceramic types that Colton and Hargrave had defined, which was made possible by the archaeological associations of tree-ring dates with pots and potsherds. Knowing when pottery types were produced allows archaeologists to assign calendar-date

Figure 6.4. Wooden beams in the roof of an ancient pit structure east of Flagstaff. Dated by A. E. Douglass in 1930, the structure produced a tree-ring date of 1142 CE.

ranges to sites that lack tree-ring dates. Ceramic dating of this sort underlies much of Southwestern archaeological chronology (plate 15).

In the 1930s and 1940s an acrimonious dispute spawned a challenge to archaeological tree-ring dating that ultimately strengthened it. The instigator was Harold S. Gladwin, founder and director of the Gila Pueblo Archaeological Foundation, a private research organization in Globe, Arizona. Gladwin, a strong believer in unilinear cultural evolution, was irritated by Colton's tree-ring-based contention that pit houses and pueblos coexisted in time. Moreover, while attending Douglass's tree-ring class at the University of Arizona, Gladwin was unable to perceive the variations in ring widths that were essential for crossdating.

Miffed on both counts, Gladwin issued publications attacking MNA's methods and reinterpreting the evidence. He set up his own tree-ring dating program, hoping to replace Douglass's qualitative method, which relied on the visual matching of ring-width patterns, with a quantitative technique employing numerical comparisons of measured ring widths.

Ultimately, Gladwin's dating method proved fatally flawed, and reanalysis of disputed tree-ring dates invariably showed his revisions to be wrong. Yet his attack did lead Douglass and Colton to thoroughly document the methods and data they had used in reaching their conclusions. They did so through published articles, monographs, and Colton's classic 1946 book, *The Sinagua: A Summary of the Archaeology of the Region of Flagstaff, Arizona.*

More important, Douglass altered the methods of recording and presenting ring-width data. Previously, tree-ring series were represented by photographs, subjective graphs, or stylized drawings. Afterward, researchers used plots of actual ring widths and standardized indices derived from them. Such quantification portrays variability in ring widths objectively and is necessary for the statistical analyses involved in reconstructing past climates. Ironically, components of Gladwin's custom-made measuring machines, which were donated to the LTRR when the Gila Pueblo Archaeological Foundation was disbanded in the 1950s, are still used at LTRR to produce accurate ring-width data.

Douglass's discovery of the relationship between ring widths in Flagstaff-area ponderosa pines and winter precipitation launched not only dendrochronology but also *dendroclimatology.* This science uses tree-ring data to calculate past variations

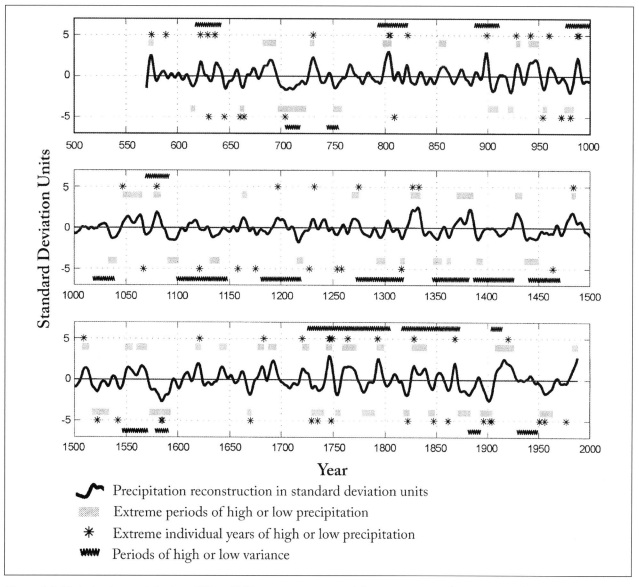

Figure 6.5. Variation in precipitation, 570 to 1988 CE, as reconstructed from tree-ring evidence. Extremely wet and dry periods and times of exceptional yearly variation in precipitation are highlighted.

in climate-related variables such as precipitation, temperature, drought, streamflow, floods, and freezes. At first researchers could identify only relative changes in climate, usually wet periods versus dry ones, by equating wet and dry years with large and small rings, respectively. In the 1960s, high-speed computers capable of handling vast amounts of data and performing countless mathematical calculations transformed dendroclimatology into the quantitative science it is today.

The American Southwest presents a difficult environment for farmers, whose crops have always been vulnerable to unevenness in rainfall and snow-fall. Douglass and his colleagues recognized early on that a sequence of unusually narrow tree rings between 1275 and 1299 in the northern Southwest represented a prolonged, severe dry spell that must have had serious repercussions for Native farmers. This dry interval coincided with important events such as the abandonment of pueblos and cliff dwellings throughout the Four Corners area, so the researchers dubbed it the Great Drought.

The obvious effects of the Great Drought tempted archaeologists to see drought as the primary cause of

Figure 6.6. Bristlecone pine tree near the summit of the San Francisco Peaks. The growth rings of bristlecone pines have been used to reconstruct ancient temperature patterns.

many cultural transformations. But they soon recognized that such transformations seldom have a single cause. Rather, they result from subtle interactions among environmental, demographic, and cultural variables. Climate, for example, in addition to heavy or scant precipitation, entails variations across time and space, trends, extremes, and events such as hailstorms and floods. Researchers began to design studies to characterize past environments more accurately in all their complexity. Dendroclimatology played a central role in this research.

In one project, the Laboratory of Tree-Ring Research built a geographical network of long, climate-sensitive tree-ring chronologies in order to calculate variability in climate over the past 2,000 years across the Southwest north of the Gila River. Quantitative reconstructions of annual precipitation for each station in the network illuminated important aspects of people's interactions with their environment across the region—not least the people of the Sierra Sin Agua.

In the late twentieth century, the Sierra Sin Agua again moved into the dendrochronological limelight as scientists tried to remedy a nagging weakness of Southwestern dendroclimatology. Ring chronologies from trees struggling to grow along the low-elevation border of the ponderosa forest are excellent indicators of rainfall, but they tell researchers little about another important factor, temperature. In the nearby Great Basin, however, the rings of bristlecone pine trees surviving along the upper tree line, where growth is limited mainly by cold, reflect variations in temperature rather than precipitation. Researchers thought similar conditions might prevail on the San Francisco Peaks, where aged bristlecone pines cling precariously to the rocky summit, defying subzero temperatures, heavy snows, and fierce winds. They constructed a timberline bristlecone chronology for the peaks, which, encouragingly, bore no resemblance to the rainfall-sensitive ponderosa sequence. Disappointingly, though, this finding was offset by the absence

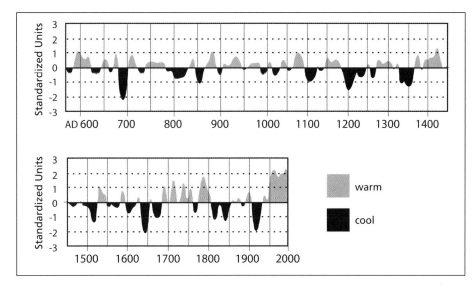

Figure 6.7. Variation through time in Flagstaff-area temperature, as reconstructed from the rings of bristlecone pine trees.

of any correlation between the bristlecone ring widths and temperature records from nearby weather stations.

In the 1990s, LTRR graduate student Matthew W. Salzer found the key to the puzzle. He established a statistical relationship between bristlecone pine ring widths and the average high temperature of the preceding year. In a bit of accidental but exquisite timing, the widening of U.S. Highway 89 north of Flagstaff provided the opportunity to pursue this exciting lead. The Tucson-based archaeological consulting firm Desert Archaeology built a dendroclimatic study into its research on archaeological sites along the highway, carried out in advance of the construction. With the new tree-ring data, Salzer was able to extend the bristlecone ring chronology back to 663 BCE, creating the first and only temperature reconstruction for the Southwest.

Comparing the temperature reconstruction with the ponderosa-based reconstruction of annual precipitation illuminates the interplay of temperature and precipitation from 570 CE to 1994. The temperature plot includes some hot, dry periods that were already well known from the precipitation chronology, such as the "Great Drought" in the late 1200s. The combined tree-ring evidence also correlates well with trends known from historical records, such as unprecedented warming after 1950 and the especially wet years of the 1980s and early 1990s. Patterns of frost-damaged bristlecone pine rings allowed Salzer to identify years in which killing frosts might have decimated crop production. These multilayered reconstructions serve as an unparalleled benchmark for evaluating humans' interactions with their environment in the Flagstaff area—work that is only just beginning.

It is no accident that the Flagstaff area nurtured so many important archaeological and denrochronological achievements. It is difficult to see how A. E. Douglass could have perfected his new science anywhere other than in the Southwestern pine forest. And without the intellectual stimulation and strong support of a local scientific community, he probably would not have become so quickly involved in so many ramifications of his method. Harold Colton's consuming interest in local prehistory impelled and guided Douglass's foray into archaeological tree-ring dating, and Colton's creation, the Museum of Northern Arizona, provided critical human, intellectual, and logistical support for the long process of building a continuous archaeological tree-ring chronology. Without exaggeration, the creation and early development of dendrochronology can be attributed to the invigorating scientific atmosphere of a time and place and its singular natural setting.

Jeffrey S. Dean is a professor emeritus of dendrochronology at the Laboratory of Tree-Ring Research at the University of Arizona.

Figure 7.1. A Navajo woman gathers plants along the Little Colorado River near Black Falls Crossing, east of Wupatki National Monument.

People and Plants in the Sierra Sin Agua

Phyllis Hogan

It is easy for modern, non-Indian people to see the Sierra Sin Agua as a vast, sunbaked landscape devoid of life, a land from which ancient people simply vanished because of drought. To Native people, however, it is a living land of great beauty, a land that sustained their ancestors for countless generations, in times of both plenty and famine. It imposes strict rules of conduct, but in exchange it provides food plants and a pharmacopoeia on which people have long depended.

Contemporary Native people living around the Sierra Sin Agua, such as the Hopis, Navajos, and Havasupais, know a great deal about how to use its plants for food, medicine, and ceremony. They gained this understanding through oral tradition, the transmission of knowledge from older relatives to younger ones. The great majority of this knowledge is ancient, hard won through the trials and errors of past generations. Native people in the region still regularly seek many of the plants used by the ancestors. They often travel to the Sierra Sin Agua to collect these plants from traditional gathering areas. Archaeologists link present knowledge to the long-ago past whenever they discover and study the remains of plants at archaeological sites.

In the Sierra Sin Agua, the landscape changes dramatically with elevation, from low, hot deserts to lofty, snowcapped peaks. Differences in elevation mean equally dramatic differences in vegetation. In the nineteenth century the biologist C. Hart Merriam observed that a 50-mile trip from the bottom of the Grand Canyon, at about 2,500 feet above sea level, to the top of the San Francisco Peaks, at more than 12,600 feet, was equivalent to traveling from the deserts of Mexico to the Arctic tundra. He characterized elevational bands displaying similar environmental conditions and vegetation as "life zones."

Because of this environmental diversity, ancient people often traveled great distances to gather food or medicinal plants in their proper seasons. Summer comes late and leaves early at the high elevations, shortening the gathering season for mountain species. In the low desert, the growing season is long, but many plants are seasonal, appearing or flowering only when temperatures warm in the spring or when rain falls in the summer. In some years, certain plants lie dormant underground in the form of seeds, biding their time until growing conditions are just right. A few plants are rare and grow in a places known only to the most knowledgeable medicine men and women.

Native people throughout the region possess vast knowledge of plants and their potential uses. Some 375 plant species grow in Wupatki National Monument alone, and of these, 122 were used in historic times for food, medicine, and religious purposes. Areas outside the monument, with different environments, support hundreds more plant species, a large number of which Native peoples also used. Before ancient people adopted agriculture, they gathered many of these plants as their

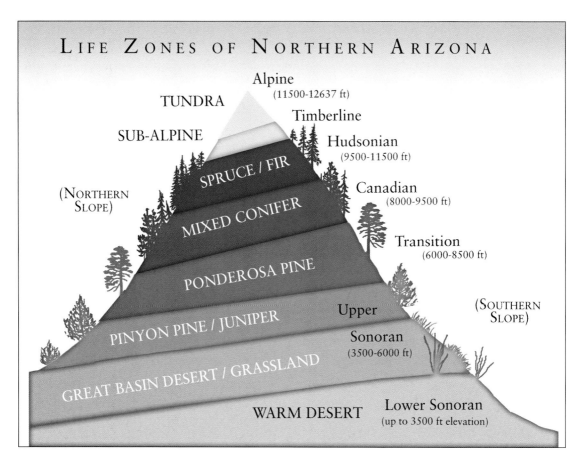

LIFE ZONES OF NORTHERN ARIZONA

Alpine
(11500-12637 ft)

TUNDRA

Timberline

SUB-ALPINE

Hudsonian
(9500-11500 ft)

SPRUCE / FIR

(NORTHERN
SLOPE)

Canadian
(8000-9500 ft)

MIXED CONIFER

Transition
(6000-8500 ft)

PONDEROSA PINE

(SOUTHERN
SLOPE)

Upper

PINYON PINE / JUNIPER

Sonoran
(3500-6000 ft)

GREAT BASIN DESERT / GRASSLAND

WARM DESERT   Lower Sonoran
(up to 3500 ft elevation)

Figure 7.2. Merriam's life zones (labels to right of schematic mountain), showing how plant communities (labels in all capitals) change with elevation in the area between the Grand Canyon and the summit of the San Francisco Peaks.

sole source of plant food. Later, wild plant foods supplemented domesticated crops.

One example of a plant used medicinally is Mormon tea, a shrub of the genus *Ephedra*. Used by all the Southwestern tribes, ephedra is among the oldest known medicinal plants. Its fibrous twigs preserve well in archaeological sites and have been found in medicine bundles—collections of plants and other objects used by Native religious specialists—dating back a thousand years or more. Mormon tea acquired that name when Native people taught Mormon settlers how to brew the twigs to make a pleasant-tasting tea, a cough medicine, and a cure for mild urinary tract infections. Strong doses of the tea act on the lungs as a bronchial dilator for respiratory problems such as asthma. Clyde Peshlakai, a respected Navajo medicine man who lived in and around what is now Wupatki National Monument, used the tea to help women during

childbirth, a unique application. Drinking the strong tea stimulated the central nervous system and gave them extra stamina.

Another example of a plant traditionally used by all tribes in the Southwest is native tobacco, a herbaceous plant with a strong odor and sticky leaves containing a high concentration of nicotine. The two species present in the Sierra Sin Agua— mountain tobacco (*Nicotiana attenuata*) and desert tobacco (*Nicotiana obtusifolia*) —both grow in rock crevices around many of the ruins at Wupatki and in the Little Colorado River basin.

To prepare native tobacco for use, people collected its leaves and dried them in the shade. They smoked tobacco in a variety of ceramic and stone pipes and occasionally in cigarette form, using sections of tubular reeds as cigarette "paper." Clyde Peshlakai blew tobacco smoke into the faces of his sheep to break their habit of running away. He also

Figure 7.3. Mormon tea (*Ephedra viridis*) growing in volcanic cinder deposits just south of Wupatki National Monument. A narrow earth crack, extending hundreds of feet below the surface, lies in the background.

purple-tinged plumes, not unlike something one might see in a Dr. Seuss children's book. It is a member of the rose family, as its aromatic flowers attest. Hopis use an infusion of the leaves to promote hair growth. Contemporary herbalists use the roots and flowers to treat coughs and make a poultice from the flowers and leaves to soothe painful joints.

Pink mallow (*Sphaeralcea* species) is a plant covered with tiny, star-shaped hairs. Its roots have a long history as a cure for stomach problems and diarrhea. Herbalists collect them in the fall, after the plant has flowered. A tea prepared from the roots is used to help heal bone fractures and sprains. Navajos prepare this tea by stripping the mucilaginous roots into shreds and then soaking them in cold water until they become sticky. Hopi people boil the entire plant and add the water to dirt that is used to seal the floors in their pueblo homes.

used the smoke any time he prayed or gave blessings to people. Traditionally, Native people smoked tobacco for prayers, to focus their thoughts, and to attract the Holy Ones. They never used it habitually and rarely recreationally.

Among other useful plants, Apache plume (*Fallugia paradoxa*) is a sprawling shrub whose white flowers give rise to large clusters of feathery,

One last example is the economically important plant lemon berry (*Rhus trilobata*), still much used today by Hopi and Navajo basket makers. Its straight, aromatic branches go into Hopi Third Mesa wicker plaques and Navajo ceremonial wedding baskets. In the late spring, people collect the plant's sticky, sour red berries and brew them into a

Figure 7.4. A modern tobacco plant, tobacco leaves, and crushed tobacco, with reed cigarettes and ceramic pipes dating from about 600 to 1250 CE.

tart, lemon-tasting beverage high in vitamin C and calcium.

Ethnobotanists—researchers who study plant use by contemporary Native people—are trained not only in anthropology, so that they understand people's cultural beliefs and practices, but also in biological taxonomy. My own interest in the plants of the Sierra Sin Agua was sparked one day in 1982 when I *didn't* know what a certain plant specimen was.

That spring, a young Navajo herbalist brought me a plant he had collected near an archaeological ruin close to his home at the Black Falls crossing on the Little Colorado River. He said the plant had many medicinal uses among Navajos, especially in the Life Way ceremony. He wanted to know what the "white man" called it—that is, its scientific name. Not recognizing the plant, I went to the herbarium at the Museum of Northern Arizona (MNA) to look it up.

As luck had it, the herbarium curator, the legendary botanist Walter McDougall, assisted me that day. He didn't have to search the pressed plant specimens housed in the herbarium cabinets; he knew the plant intimately.

"*Amsonia peeblesii*," he said triumphantly, identifying the plant commonly known as Peebles blue star. He also knew that it must have come from one particular ruin in Wupatki National Monument. McDougall's familiarity with the plant resulted from the three years he had spent studying plant specimens in the monument.

Later that spring a U.S. National Park Service (NPS) ranger came to visit me, bringing with him a plant he wanted identified. He had seen local Navajos collecting it near a ruin in Wupatki National Monument and hoped I could identify it and shed light on why the Navajos wanted it. NPS was gathering information about how Native people used natural resources in parks, in order to determine whether picking and collecting should be allowed at all. The strict rules regarding protection of natural resources on park land made collecting without a permit a federal offense.

This time I knew immediately that the plant he showed me was *Amsonia peeblesii*. It is a rare species that grows in only a few isolated places in northern Arizona—and it seems to flourish at Wupatki.

Western Navajo herbalists treasure the plant, especially the roots, for healing, and the Wupatki Basin was a traditional collecting area. I explained to the ranger that the area around one of the ruins was the only easily accessible place in the region where local Navajo people knew to find Peebles blue star.

The plants from this site also had spiritual significance, because in Navajo oral tradition the Wupatki area was where Asdzáá Nadleehe, Ever-Changing Woman, first instructed Navajo people in how to use *Amsonia*. The benevolent figure of Asdzáá Nadleehe rests at the core of Navajo healing philosophy and religion. She is the Navajo earth mother and goddess of vegetation, the main deity associated with plant life. It was she who brought the theory of the Blessing Way—the seeking of harmony with all that exists—into the Navajo healing system. Plants are infused with sacred significance because they belong to her.

The ranger explained to me that in spite of the importance of the site and its tradition of use, his agency had a duty to protect all resources in the monument's jurisdiction. Given this, we consulted with local people to search for an alternative gathering area where Navajos could obtain the plants they needed without running afoul of the federal government. Fortunately, we found a large population of *Amsonia peeblesii* growing on private land just beyond the monument's boundaries. Working with the landowner, we gained permission for local people to harvest small amounts of the plant every year. Everyone was satisfied. Additionally, NPS agreed to facilitate access to the ruins by Navajo herbalists, so they could make prayer offerings to the plant.

As an ethnobotanist, I was pleased to be able to serve as a bridge of cultural understanding between the federal government and Navajo people. The experience also made me feel connected to the vast knowledge about plants that extends from ancient times—as attested by the remains of plants at archaeological sites—to contemporary Native people.

Of course the most important and knowledgeable scholars of plants and their uses are the Native people who carry the knowledge of their ancestors. Clyde Peshlakai was one such expert. Born in 1888 at Black Point, on the Navajo reservation near Wupatki National Monument, to Baa (his mother, given the name Vera Standish) and Peshlakai Etsidi, Clyde was a prominent *nataanii*, or headman, a talented silversmith, and a skilled herbalist and ceremonial practitioner, as his father had been. His family had deep roots in the area. During the late eighteenth century, small groups of Navajo families hunted for game and gathered plants around the Wupatki Basin and the Coconino Plateau. By the 1930s, four extended family groups had settled permanently there and in the lower Little Colorado River corridor, all of them descended from Clyde's father.

As an herbalist, Clyde Peshlakai's ceremonial repertoire encompassed a tremendous amount of esoteric knowledge, because specific protocols are required even before a plant is collected. Navajo teachings recognize that the earth and everything connected with it—land, air, light, moisture, plants, and animals—are an integrated system of life and have an inner life form similar to that of humans. Like other Native peoples, Navajos do not regard plants as a commodity. The first and foremost lesson of the aspiring Navajo herbalist is the proper way to address the spirit of the plants and to behave when collecting or preparing plants for healing. The plant people are obligated to accept an offering of corn pollen placed at the base of a medicinal plant. The plant will help restore a patient's health when proper introductions are made.

The ethnobotanical knowledge of this region will live on as long as people make use of the plants and the ancient knowledge about them that has been handed down across the generations. The plants of the Sierra Sin Agua are more than just a collection of botanical species—they are a living pharmacy in the middle of a seemingly lifeless desert.

Figure 7.5. Clyde Peshlakai, in 1936, during his tenure as an NPS ranger at Wupatki National Monument.

Phyllis Hogan has been a practicing Southwestern herbalist for more than 25 years. Her Winter Sun Trading Company, in Flagstaff, Arizona, specializes in traditional organic Southwestern herbs as well as American Indian art. In 1983 Hogan co-founded the nonprofit Arizona Ethnobotanical Research Association to investigate, document, and preserve traditional plant use in Arizona and the greater Southwest.

Plate 1. *Top right:* Paleoindian projectile points from the Sierra Sin Agua. *Top row, three left-most:* Clovis points; others are later styles.

Plate 2. *Bottom left:* An atlatl (right) and stone-tipped fore-shafts for darts, from Sand Dune Cave, Utah. Although they date from the first century CE, they illustrate important parts of the hunting technology used by earlier Paleoindian and Archaic peoples of the Sierra Sin Agua.

Plate 3. *Bottom right:* Split-twig animal figurines, probably representing deer or antelope, from Walnut Canyon. Such objects may have been used during late Archaic times as symbols of group identity or as totems in rituals promoting hunting success.

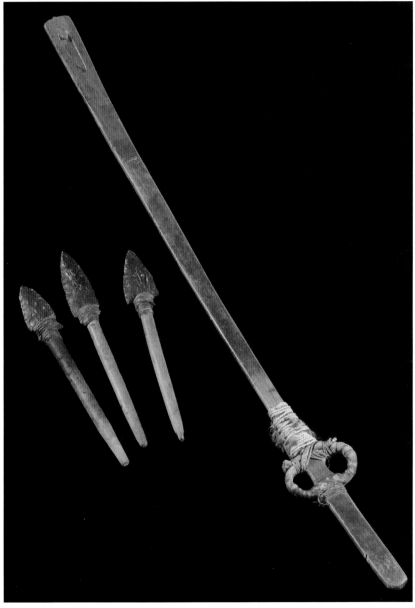

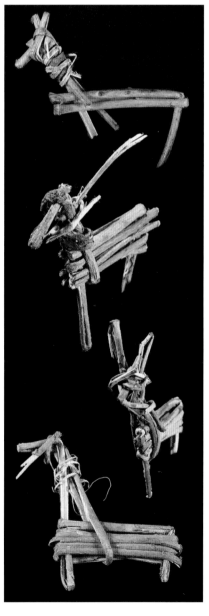

Plate 4. A large, circular room crudely built of basalt on Sunset Crater cinders, south of Wupatki National Monument. Such rooms, of unknown function, often appear adjacent to pueblos. The San Francisco Peaks rise in the background.

Plate 5. Aerial view of an unnamed, unexcavated, twelfth-century pueblo in the Coconino National Forest, south of Wupatki National Monument.

Plate 6. Lomaki Ruin at Wupatki National Monument, looking south toward the San Francisco Peaks.

Plate 7. Aerial view of Medicine Fort, a site about four miles west-northwest of Sunset Crater. Massive walls of basalt and scoria, up to four feet thick, outline a central courtyard and a row of narrow rooms.

Plate 8. Petroglyphs of abstract geometric designs, spirals, pottery designs, and anthropomorphs on the lower slopes of a basalt mesa near Citadel Pueblo at Wupatki National Monument.

Plate 9. A tightly wrapped, rayed spiral pecked on a sandstone boulder near Crack-in-Rock Pueblo at Wupatki National Monument.

Plate 10. Zoomorphic figures and what appears to be a footprint—perhaps of a bear—adorning a basalt outcrop at Anderson Pass. View is northwest across the piñon-juniper woodland east of Flagstaff.

Plate 11. Artist's conception of the interior of a Winona Village pit house as it might have looked at sunrise in the early autumn, about 1130 CE. Based on site NA3644C, excavated by the Museum of Northern Arizona in the late 1930s.

Plate 12. Archaeologists excavating an "alcove" pit house (foreground) and a rectangular, stone-lined pit house in southeastern Flagstaff, Arizona. Elden Mountain is visible to the north.

Plate 13. Little Box Canyon Pueblo, in Wupatki National Monument. Its doorway, once open as shown in plate 14, was sealed with rock sometime during the later occupation of the site.

Plate 14. Artist's conception of Little Box Canyon Pueblo as it might have looked in late summer, about 1190 CE. View is from an angle slightly different from that in plate 13.

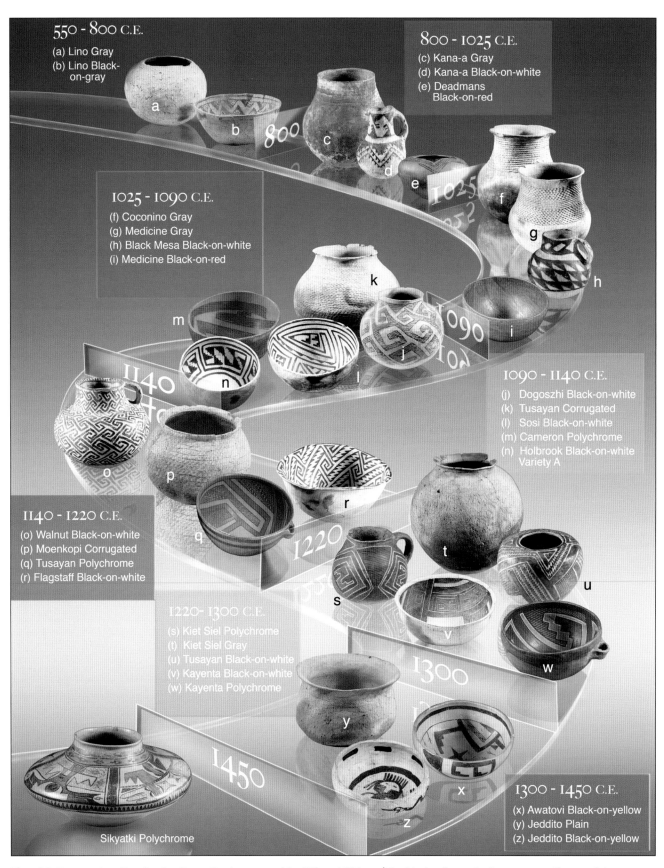

550 - 800 C.E.
(a) Lino Gray
(b) Lino Black-on-gray

800 - 1025 C.E.
(c) Kana-a Gray
(d) Kana-a Black-on-white
(e) Deadmans Black-on-red

1025 - 1090 C.E.
(f) Coconino Gray
(g) Medicine Gray
(h) Black Mesa Black-on-white
(i) Medicine Black-on-red

1090 - 1140 C.E.
(j) Dogoszhi Black-on-white
(k) Tusayan Corrugated
(l) Sosi Black-on-white
(m) Cameron Polychrome
(n) Holbrook Black-on-white Variety A

1140 - 1220 C.E.
(o) Walnut Black-on-white
(p) Moenkopi Corrugated
(q) Tusayan Polychrome
(r) Flagstaff Black-on-white

1220 - 1300 C.E.
(s) Kiet Siel Polychrome
(t) Kiet Siel Gray
(u) Tusayan Black-on-white
(v) Kayenta Black-on-white
(w) Kayenta Polychrome

1300 - 1450 C.E.
(x) Awatovi Black-on-yellow
(y) Jeddito Plain
(z) Jeddito Black-on-yellow

Sikyatki Polychrome

Plate 15. Pottery time line for the Sierra Sin Agua, roughly 550 to 1500 CE. The kinds of vessels shown were all part of the Kayenta ancestral pueblo and Hopi ceramic traditions, centered just to the east and north of the Sierra Sin Agua.

Plate 16. Two large jars unearthed from a cinder dune near an archaeological site northwest of Sunset Crater. *Left:* San Francisco Mountain Gray Ware (type Deadmans Fugitive Red); *right:* Tusayan White Ware (type Sosi Black-on-white). The vessels were imported from manufacturing zones at least 130 miles apart.

Plate 17. Alameda Brown Ware vessels, including bowls with polished interiors and jars with corrugated exteriors.

Plate 18. San Juan Red Ware and Tsegi Orange Ware vessels.

Plate 19. Potsherds found at Wupatki National Monument, representing pottery making from about 750 to 1250 CE. Most came from vessels made far from Wupatki and imported into the area.

Plate 20. A Tusayan Gray Ware (Kana'a Gray) jar dating to around 950 CE, with balls of yucca twine that were found stored inside it.

Plate 21. Pots and potsherds from the Sierra Sin Agua. Large jars, *left to right:* Tusayan Corrugated, Deadmans Fugitive Red, Sunset Red. Ladle: Tusayan Polychrome. Bowl: Flagstaff Black-on-white.

Plate 22. Close-up of Tusayan Polychrome vessel design.

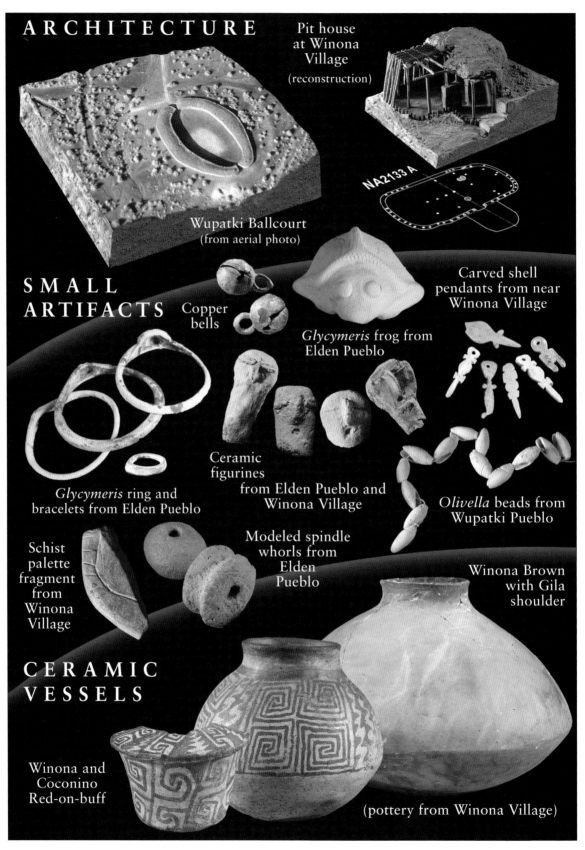

ARCHITECTURE

Pit house
at Winona
Village

(reconstruction)

NA2133 A

Wupatki Ballcourt
(from aerial photo)

**SMALL
ARTIFACTS**

Copper
bells

Carved shell
pendants from near
Winona Village

Glycymeris frog from
Elden Pueblo

Ceramic
figurines
from Elden Pueblo and
Winona Village

Glycymeris ring and
bracelets from Elden Pueblo

Olivella beads from
Wupatki Pueblo

Schist
palette
fragment
from
Winona
Village

Modeled spindle
whorls from
Elden
Pueblo

Winona Brown
with Gila
shoulder

**CERAMIC
VESSELS**

Winona and
Coconino
Red-on-buff

(pottery from Winona Village)

Plate 23. Material evidence for Hohokam presence or influence found in the Sierra Sin Agua. The architecture, small artifacts, and pottery all have analogs in the Hohokam area surrounding Phoenix, Arizona.

Plate 24. Modern specimens and replicas of ancient exotic items exchanged in the Sierra Sin Agua, showing their original brilliant colors. Pictured are marine shells, mineralized sand dollars, macaw feathers, cotton (in small pottery jar at upper right), minerals, ground pigments (in shell containers), copper bells (bottom center), turquoise, salt (in small pottery bowl below feathers), argillite, hematite, obsidian, and jet.

Plate 25. Carved pendants of abalone (*Haliotis*) shell from a site near Winona Village dating to around 1090–1130 CE, shown with modern, unworked *Haliotis* shells.

Plate 26. Carved pendants of *Laevicardium* shell, displayed against a modern, unworked *Laevicardium* specimen. From Elden Pueblo and a site near Winona Village, around 1090–1300 CE.

Plate 27. Turquoise pendants, beads, and mosaic pieces mostly from Elden Pueblo, dating between about 1070 and 1300 CE.

Plate 28. Nose plugs of argillite and limestone, fitted with end pieces of limestone, hematite, travertine, and turquoise, mostly from Elden Pueblo, about 1070–1300 CE.

Plate 29. Nose plugs, lip plug, pendants, and beads of argillite, mostly from Elden Pueblo, about 1070–1300 CE.

Plate 30. Copper bells from archaeological sites in the Sierra Sin Agua, about 1070–1130 CE.

Figure 8.1. Artist's conception of Pleistocene animals—a bison (*Bison antiquus*) and a mammoth (*Mammuthus columbii*)—at a seasonal watering hole in today's Wupatki National Monument, around 11,000 BCE. The San Francisco Peaks are visible at far right, their summits blanketed in snow. Sunset Crater volcano does not appear on the skyline, because it has not yet erupted at this time.

Motisinom

Ancient Peoples from Pleistocene to Pueblo

Francis E. Smiley and Michael J. Novotny

Long before the ancient people known to the Hopis as Hisat'sinom became settled farmers and built stable pit house and pueblo communities, an original group of inhabitants roamed the Sierra Sin Agua. The Hopis call these people Motisinom, the truly ancient ones. In the beginning the Motisinom were nomadic, moving with the seasons, gathering wild plant foods and hunting big game. Their way of life spanned thousands of years, beginning with the last ice age, but it left few material traces. We must piece together their story from clues scattered thinly over a vast landscape.

Archaeologists call the earliest Motisinom "Paleoindians." These hunters lived in North America by the final stage of the most recent ice age, which lasted from about 125,000 to about 10,000 years ago. During that time, much of what is now Canada and the northern United States lay beneath sheets of ice up to two miles thick. Many giant mammals and birds—"megafauna"—roamed the landscape, including mammoths, mastodons, lions, camels, piglike animals, sabertooth cats, ground sloths, and condorlike birds with wing spans of more than 16 feet. Toward the end of that time, the world's climate was warming, and the glaciers were melting and retreating.

To understand the Paleoindians of the Sierra Sin Agua, archaeologists labor under what we like to call the "tyranny of projectile points." That is, almost the only traces these ancient hunters left in the area are whole and broken examples of their stone hunting tools and the waste flakes left over from making them. Skillfully they fashioned large, beautifully flaked, pointed tools that probably served as lance or dart heads, as well as sharp knives and scrapers. Elsewhere in the Southwest such tools sometimes cluster on the ground surface, marking places where early nomads camped or lay in wait for game. In the Sierra Sin Agua we find them only in isolation, one at a time, at spots where hunters lost whole tools or, more often, discarded broken ones.

Researchers have worked out sequences of projectile point styles on the basis of changing sizes, shapes, and manufacturing techniques. They have been able to date these point types by radiocarbon analyses of charcoal from burned plants found in the same geological layers as the artifacts. So far no evidence suggests that anyone lived in the American Southwest before about 13,500 years ago. In the Sierra Sin Agua the earliest signs of human presence are points characteristic of the so-called Clovis culture, named for an archaeological site near Clovis, New Mexico, where this distinctive weapon was first found. The people archaeologists call Clovis existed from about 13,125 to 12,925 years ago.

Clovis points are usually large and always well made. A large flake removed from the base on one or both sides forms a channel called a "flute" (plate 1). Experiments have shown that by thinning the point, a flute enhances its ability to penetrate far enough into an animal's body to cause a lethal

Figure 8.2. Projectile points from the Flagstaff area. At center is a Clovis point, enlarged to show details, dating to around 11,000 BCE, which archaeologists found on the ground surface about a mile from the place depicted in figure 8.1. Surrounding points span the Paleoindian through Late Archaic periods.

wound. Hunters likely attached Clovis points to the ends of darts by means of a small foreshaft that fitted into a longer main shaft. That way a hunter could reload the main shaft repeatedly after the foreshaft found its target and the main shaft fell to the ground. Clovis darts, like later ones for many centuries, were probably propelled with an atlatl, a kind of handheld lever that rotated around the base of a dart's main shaft to give it greater velocity and accuracy (plate 2). Modern experiments have verified that Clovis points were ideal for killing large game, especially mammoths.

Clovis people were skilled hunters and gatherers who traveled in small groups spread sparsely across the landscape. At excavated sites elsewhere in the Southwest, their distinctive projectile points appear consistently with the bones of slain mammoths. They also occasionally hunted smaller game and gathered wild plant foods, but evidence for these activities is scant. Clovis people lived in small, largely egalitarian societies, probably practiced shamanistic religions, and moved frequently to track game animals and seasonal changes in wild plant resources. We know from excavations in southeastern Arizona that Clovis people occasionally gathered in small camps near mammoth kills, but so far no such sites have been found in the Sierra Sin Agua. Perhaps some lie buried beneath the thick layers of soil that have accumulated in arroyos and river bottoms during the nearly 13,000 years since Clovis culture ended.

Evidence from geology, ancient pollen, and buried animal bones, among other sources, tells us that as the ice age drew to a close during the brief span of Clovis culture, the Southwestern climate was relatively warm and very dry. Streams ran lower than at any time in the preceding 20,000 years, and surface water apparently was scarce. These drought conditions, paradoxically, might have helped Clovis hunters, drawing animals to gather around the few watering holes, where they were easier to find and ambush.

Abruptly, the megafauna went extinct, and the tools that define Clovis culture disappeared. Both events apparently came about when the Northern Hemisphere plunged into a 1,300-year period of cold, wet climate known as the Younger Dryas. This climate shift is marked geologically by a peculiar layer of dark sediment known as the "black mat." Though only a few inches thick, black mat deposits can be found all across North America and in Europe as far east as Germany. They date consistently to about 12,900 years ago. Many Clovis sites lie under the black mat, and no Clovis remains or

Pleistocene megafauna have been discovered above it. Black mat sediments formed in the presence of water, and indeed, water tables rose rapidly in the Southwest during the Younger Dryas. Some Clovis campsites in parts of the Southwest other than the Sierra Sin Agua became waterlogged, which preserved them well.

A truly remarkable new development on the Clovis scene in the Flagstaff region is the discovery of a large Clovis-era camp under investigation by archaeologists from Northern Arizona University. The newly recognized Rainbow Forest Site lies in the southwestern portion of Petrified Forest National Park about 100 miles east of Flagstaff. The Rainbow Forest Site surrounds a small playa lake that fills seasonally with rainwater. Petrified Forest National Park is justly famous for a landscape covered with petrified wood. The petrified wood supply was likely a major draw for Clovis and later populations in the area. The Clovis artisans made spear points and a range of other distinctive stone tools from the petrified wood, often heat-treating the wood in campfires to make it more workable.

The true importance of the Rainbow Forest Site lies in the fact that it is the only actual Clovis camp site known on the southern Colorado Plateau. All other Clovis evidence consists entirely of isolated projectile points, such as the one in figure 8.2. Although the Clovis era ended suddenly, prehistoric populations continued to frequent the Rainbow Forest Site for thousands of years. The site has also produced Folsom projectile points and tools as well as artifacts from the Early Archaic.

The end of Clovis culture, whatever its causes, by no means ended the nomadic, hunting way of life. What archaeologists recognize as the Paleoindian period endured, with changes, for almost another 4,000 years. After Clovis times, people across western North America began making a new type of projectile point, now famously known as the Folsom point—again for its place of discovery, near Folsom, New Mexico. Motisinom people used Folsom points to hunt one of the few species of megafauna to survive into this era, a now-extinct large bison. We rarely find these points in northern Arizona, which suggests that their makers were few and lived in widely scattered bands.

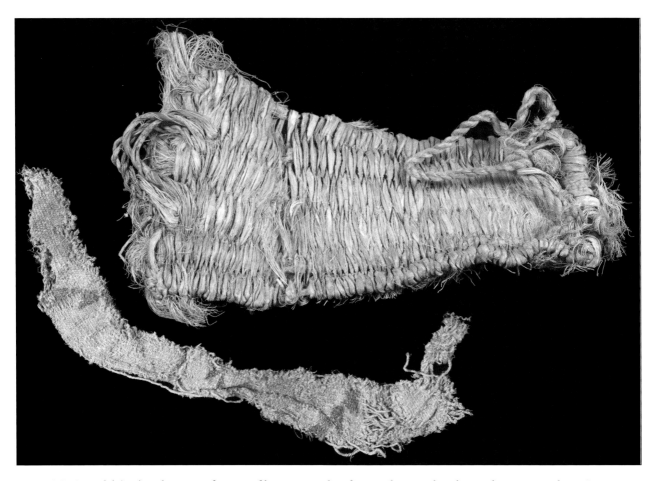

Figure 8.3. A sandal (top) and a piece of a yucca fiber carrying bag from early agricultural period sites in northern Arizona.

As the climate again began to warm up and dry out after the Younger Dryas, the Folsom culture—at least as defined by its projectile points—faded away, and the point-making traditions of Paleoindians in western North America began to diverge. Archaeologists recognize many such traditions by the sizes and shapes of their dart points, to which they have given names such as Midland, Agate Basin, Eden, and Hell Gap, each characterizing a particular region at a particular time. Some of these later Paleoindians, too, ranged across the Sierra Sin Agua, living in small bands and traveling great distances to pursue game animals such as the deer, elk, bison, and pronghorn antelope we know today.

About 9,000 years ago, lifeways across North America began to change, to the extent that archaeologists consider the Paleoindian era to have given way to the so-called Archaic period. The Archaic was a time of global warming following the ice-bound Pleistocene. People began to shift from the late Paleoindian reliance on hunting bison and other large game to a more mixed economy in which they gathered diverse plant foods and hunted animals both large and small. They probably moved seasonally, following the yearly movements of game and the ripening of plant foods such as piñon nuts, an important, storable source of protein and fat.

In many places in the Southwest, archaeologists have found stone mortars and pestles that people used to grind seeds at Archaic campsites. Occasionally, Archaic-period sandals, ropes, baskets, and other normally perishable items—everything from snares and nets to hide clothing and human feces—turn up preserved in dry caves. But in the Sierra Sin Agua we know the Archaic Motisinom only in the way we know their Paleoindian predecessors—through their points and stone flakes.

Like Paleoindian points, early Archaic ones served as dart points used in conjunction with atlatls; the bow and arrow did not appear until

Figure 8.4. Early Archaic projectile points from the Sierra Sin Agua.

roughly 500 CE. Early Archaic points are smaller than Paleoindian forms. The many later named types—Sudden Side-notched, Pinto–San Jose, Gypsum Cave, Gatecliff Split-stemmed, and Elko Eared, for example—grew successively smaller, probably because people increasingly hunted more small game such as rabbits and hares. And unlike isolated Paleoindian points, Archaic points and debris from stone tool manufacturing sometimes appear in clusters, marking places where people camped for a while.

In some rock shelters and caves on the southern Colorado Plateau, late Archaic people left behind small, split-twig effigies of game animals. Perhaps they intended these as offerings to increase success in hunting expeditions or as symbols of social identity. In the Sierra Sin Agua, archaeologists have discovered numerous split twig figurines in the vicinity of Walnut Canyon (plate 3).

Late in the Archaic period, between about 4,600 and 1,600 years ago, projectile point styles proliferated throughout the Southwest, suggesting that

people were diversifying culturally. Archaeologists find larger numbers of these points, too, so they believe the population was growing. With more people on the landscape, groups might now have been restricted to smaller territories than their ancestors had available. In addition, the late Archaic was warmer and generally wetter than earlier Archaic times. This made plant growth more reliable and abundant, so people no longer had to travel so far to feed themselves. They began to settle for longer times near permanent water and important, dependable food sources such as piñon trees. Studies of the locations where Archaic points have been found in the Sierra Sin Agua show that these generalizations hold true for that area just as for other parts of the Southwest.

As late Archaic people began to live more settled lives and depend more heavily on local food sources, they may have been predisposed to adopt the growing of maize and squash, which had been domesticated centuries earlier in what is now Mexico, once those plants were introduced to the region. Farming did not come to the Sierra Sin Agua until relatively late in the Southwestern sequence, probably around 400 CE, according to radiocarbon dates for prehistoric maize recently excavated just north of Flagstaff.

With the shift from hunting and gathering to agriculture came profound changes in virtually every aspect of ancient life. Within a couple of centuries or so, landscapes surrounding the San Francisco Peaks were home to pottery-using people who lived in many small hamlets of scattered pit houses, cultivating crops introduced to the region by their ancestors. By the early 1100s, descendants of these early farmers had begun building above-ground pueblos, setting the stage for rapid cultural changes that would culminate in large, diverse communities such as Wupatki, Elden, and Turkey Hill Pueblos. With these developments, the long journey from Pleistocene to pueblo was complete.

Francis E. Smiley is a professor of anthropology at Northern Arizona University. His research interests range from lithic analysis to archaeological chronometry, computer simulation, and geographic information systems, but his primary focus has been small-scale societies and the transition to agriculture.

Michael J. Novotny is an archaeologist who specializes in lithic analysis and the use of technology to map Southwestern archaeological sites.

Figure 8.5. Middle Archaic projectile points from the Coconino National Forest.

Figure 8.6. Late Archaic projectile points.

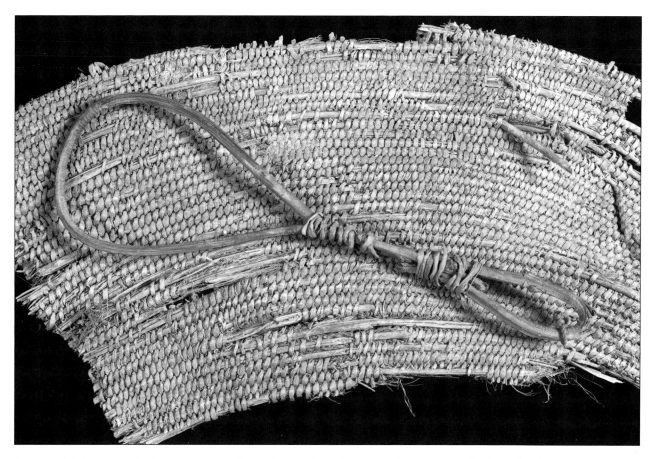

Figure 8.7. A fragment of a large, traylike basket and a small wooden object that people probably used to beat the seed heads of grasses or weedy plants, driving the seeds into the basket. Early agricultural period, northern Arizona.

Figure 9.1. Hohokam ball court at Wupatki Pueblo (top) and Chaco-style stone masonry at Ridge Ruin. *Inset:* details of Chaco-style masonry, with small chinking stones interspersed among carefully shaped wall stones.

Hohokam and Chaco in the Sierra Sin Agua

nine

F. Michael O'Hara

In ancient times the Sierra Sin Agua formed a major cultural crossroads. Several trade routes converged there, bringing valued items from distant corners of the Southwest. Perhaps more important, the Sierra Sin Agua witnessed the intersection of two of the Southwest's great cultural systems. One, known as Hohokam, flourished between about 450 and 1450 CE in the Sonoran Desert of present-day southern Arizona. At its peak, Hohokam society encompassed a network of large villages featuring mounds used as dance platforms, Mexican-style ball courts where teams played ceremonial games, and agricultural fields watered by a grid of sophisticated irrigation canals.

The other great system developed in Chaco Canyon, in the San Juan River basin of northwestern New Mexico, beginning around 850 CE. At its zenith of economic power and cultural influence, between about 1035 and 1080, the Chacoan network of massive, dominating stone pueblos, called "great houses," and large, underground ceremonial rooms, or great kivas, had spread across much of the Colorado Plateau. Nowhere did these two traditions overlap to such a degree as in the Sierra Sin Agua.

The results are tangible at Hisat'sinom ruins in many ways. Wupatki Pueblo, for example, has both a Hohokam-style ball court and a Chaco-like great kiva. Local communities such as Winona Village and Ridge Ruin also show eclectic blends of architectural features, artifact styles, and cultural practices such as methods of burying the dead.

After decades of research, archaeologists still struggle to understand what happened here, and why local archaeological remains reflect such a blend of the surrounding region's styles and cultural practices. One thing seems certain: the Hisat'sinom of the Sierra Sin Agua were not dominated by either Hohokam or Chaco, but rather crafted their own unique cultural amalgam.

Relationships with Hohokam people began early in the Sierra Sin Agua, decades or even centuries before the Sunset Crater volcano erupted in the late eleventh century. The "Hohokam connection" manifests itself in Hohokam architectural forms such as pit houses and ball courts, imported Hohokam artifacts, locally made versions of Hohokam items, and the adoption of Hohokam burial practices (plate 23). The intensity and duration of the connection suggests that it went beyond mere trade ties. Some archaeologists have suggested that Hohokam people themselves moved into the area along with their trade goods. Others vigorously dispute this.

Hohokam-style ball courts appear throughout the Sierra Sin Agua as oval depressions in the ground outlined by earthen berms along the long axis. Usually, small steps lead down to the court's interior from narrow openings at either end. The courts often have "end markers"—one or more small stones either protruding slightly above the floor or sealed beneath it—and sometimes markers in the center of the floor as well. The few excavated ball courts in the Flagstaff area have carefully plastered

Figure 9.2. Aerial view of Ridge Ruin, showing twin ball courts downslope from the main pueblo.

floors, often showing evidence of multiple replasterings, perhaps repairs necessitated by the harsh, wet winters at this high elevation.

Many archaeologists believe people used these structures as arenas for a ball game like that played in Mesoamerica and western Mexico. In a widespread Mesoamerican tradition, these games reenacted a cosmic contest between mortals and gods and helped regulate relationships between communities through competitions constrained by rules and ritual. Ball courts might also have been important social venues for trade among communities, ensuring regular, peaceful interactions.

So far archaeologists have found 13 ball courts in the Flagstaff area, concentrated in two locations: a 7-mile stretch of Deadman Wash northeast of the San Francisco Peaks and a 15-mile, west-to-east line paralleling the Rio de Flag and the San Francisco Wash to the south. Eleven ball courts date from about 1090 to 1140 CE, and two earlier ones apparently

belong to the century before Sunset Crater erupted. Most communities had only a single ball court, but Ridge Ruin had two. Curiously, one of them showed evidence of a large, upright post in the center, a feature not documented for ball courts in other areas.

What forces brought ball courts to the Sierra Sin Agua is unknown, but the tradition likely spread from the adjacent Verde Valley. Hohokam-style ball courts appeared there just before the first ball courts in the Flagstaff area. The latter might have linked the people of the Sierra Sin Agua into the larger Hohokam trade network via a strong Hohokam cultural tradition in the Verde Valley.

In 1938 and 1939, archaeologists from the Museum of Northern Arizona (MNA) excavated Winona Village, some 15 miles east of Flagstaff, because the site held the first ball court to be identified in the Flagstaff area. Unlike most pre eruption sites, which consist of only a handful of houses, Winona had as many as 36 pit houses and a three-room, above-ground pueblo. Whereas earlier settlements usually housed only a single extended family apiece, Winona Village accommodated several groups who might have been unrelated or perhaps related only through marriage. Each group maintained its own social space, as was shown by distinct clusters of pit houses with associated trash deposits.

From the wide range of architectural forms at Winona Village, Harold Colton and other researchers at MNA defined sequential but overlapping cultural patterns, which they called "foci"— Angell, Winona, and Padre—for the immediate post-eruption period, 1080 to 1140. They believed these foci represented arrivals in the area of immigrants from surrounding regions, including Hohokam immigrants from the south. They believed the variability of house forms at Winona Village resulted from local people living side by side with newcomers from elsewhere.

Several Hohokam-like pit houses are known in the Flagstaff area, almost all of them at sites with ball courts, including one, site NA2133A, that overlooks the ball court at Winona Village. Tree-ring dates indicate that people lived in this house from about 1086 to 1095 CE. The structure burned with a large number of whole pots and other artifacts on the floor, as did four other excavated, Hohokam-style pit houses in the area. Questions about these houses have stumped archaeologists for decades: Who lived in them? Hohokam immigrants? Local residents who suddenly adopted many Hohokam customs? Long-distance traders who lived briefly in the Sierra Sin Agua? Visiting ritual specialists who directed ball games?

Besides ball courts and pit houses, people of the Sierra Sin Agua adopted three other aspects of Hohokam culture: cremation of the dead, Hohokam vessel forms and decorative styles in red-on-buff pottery, and the manufacture and exchange of marine shell ornaments. The first two appeared after the Sunset Crater eruption and lasted for only two or three generations. Trade in shells and other exotic goods began earlier and lasted for as long as Hisat'sinom lived in the Sierra Sin Agua, until roughly 1200 CE.

The few human remains excavated from pre-eruption sites in the area almost invariably come from inhumations, or burials of the bodies of the dead. After the eruption people began commonly to cremate the dead. Social groups also began creating formal cemeteries, places where they repeatedly disposed of their deceased members. Archaeologists who study mortuary practices suggest that formal cemeteries mark increasing recognition of distinct social groups and their ownership of land or other resources. Ancestral relations commemorated through mortuary rituals validate political and economic claims. Mortuary rituals bring related people together to mend the social fabric torn by the loss of a group member. Relationships are reaffirmed, and the social roles and material property of the deceased are distributed to the appropriate surviving members.

At Winona Village, many of the pit house clusters lie adjacent to features that archaeologists have called trash mounds. But these mounds, 30 to 50 feet in diameter and 3 feet or more high, do not appear represent the gradual accumulation of household trash. People placed both bodies and cremated remains in or adjacent to them. I believe these mounds were deliberately constructed, perhaps beginning with spoil from the excavation of pit houses and then augmented with household trash, to serve as cemeteries. People might have performed funerary rites on their elevated surfaces.

One pit house cluster at the northern end of Winona Village features a mound with an adjacent cremation cemetery. Usually, bodies of the dead were burned in one place, and the ashes buried in another, often inside a pot. Occasionally, people left the cremated remains and associated offerings where they had burned, often in an area defined archaeologically by four postholes. These treatments and the arrangement of mounds and cemetery features resemble those found at Hohokam sites in the Phoenix area.

Evidence from Winona and other sites suggests that different social groups used different mortuary treatments. Usually a mound contains mostly or exclusively either cremations or inhumations, and often a nearby mound shows the opposite pattern. In one cluster of houses at Winona Village, for example, one mound held 73 percent cremations, whereas a neighboring mound contained only inhumations.

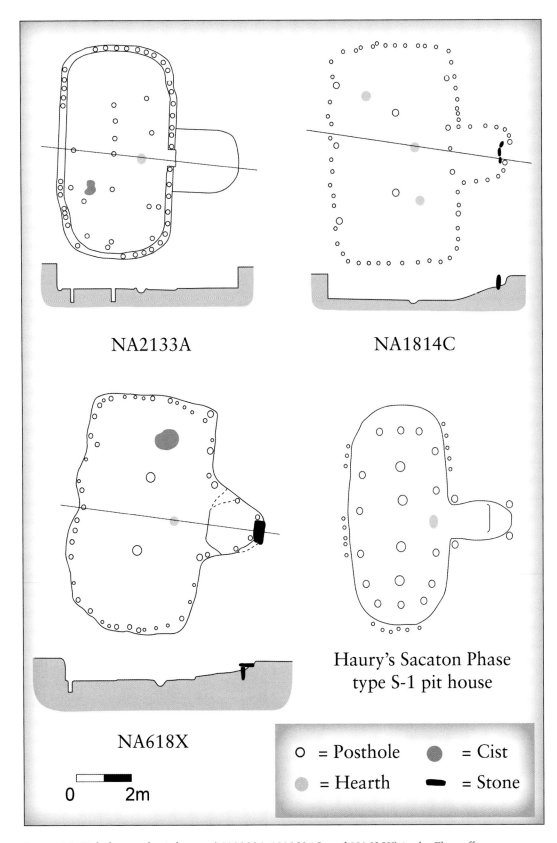

NA2133A

NA1814C

NA618X

Haury's Sacaton Phase
type S-1 pit house

○ = Posthole   ● = Cist

● = Hearth   ▬ = Stone

0   2m

Figure 9.3. Hohokam-style pit houses (NA2133A, NA1814C, and NA618X) in the Flagstaff area, compared with a true Hohokam pit house (lower right) from the site of Snaketown, just south of modern Phoenix, Arizona. All four structures date between about 1070 and 1130 CE.

Figure 9.4. A thick-walled censer from Winona Village. This locally made example is nearly identical to Hohokam censers from the Phoenix Basin. The purpose of these vessels remains unknown.

This patterning might mean that treatment of the dead corresponded to a group's ethnicity or social identity, perhaps within a dual division of society.

Turning to pottery, we can see Hohokam influence in the Sierra Sin Agua in the form of locally produced pots painted with red designs on a buff-colored background, closely similar to Hohokam pottery. Some vessels have distinctive Hohokam pottery shapes as well. These include censers—heavy, solid vessels with a bowl in the top. Like their Hohokam counterparts, the censers display a pattern of sooting and oxidation suggesting use as incense burners. Some jars take a distinctive form known as the "Gila shoulder" that is commonly found in Hohokam pottery (plate 23).

At Winona Village, trash deposits produced pieces of both locally produced red-on-buff vessels and pots imported from the Hohokam heartland itself. The clay in the local pottery incorporated volcanic cinders and tuff as "temper," which helps prevent the clay from cracking as it dries. The Hohokam pottery was tempered with micaceous schist from the middle Gila River, south of present-day Phoenix. The locally produced red-on-buff designs were nearly identical to designs on Hohokam pottery but quite unlike the designs used on Pueblo-style black-on-white pottery from the same deposits. A few fired clay figurines, some resembling Hohokam

examples from the Phoenix area, also appear at Winona and other Flagstaff-area sites.

Besides importing some of their pottery from their neighbors, the people of the Sierra Sin Agua benefited from living at a nexus of two trading routes that gave them access to marine shells and jewelry made from it—bracelets, necklaces, and pendants. Ancient trails leading west across the Mohave Desert to the Pacific Ocean followed roughly the path of historic Route 66 and modern Interstate 40. To the south, trails passed through the Hohokam heartland and on to the Gulf of California (see fig. 19.2). The amount of shell acquired by residents of the Sierra Sin Agua via the Hohokam route increased greatly after the eruption of Sunset Crater, coincident with the increase in the number of local ball courts and other Hohokam cultural items and practices.

At least some people of the Sierra Sin Agua produced Hohokam-style shell jewelry themselves, rather than just acquiring it ready-made. At Winona Village, excavators found fragments of shell debris from jewelry manufacturing, suggesting that people living in ball court villages had access to sources of raw shell and were well versed in the techniques and forms associated with Hohokam shell jewelry.

Research by Tracy Murphy (see chapter 19) has demonstrated that the distribution of shell jewelry

Figure 9.5. Fired clay figurines from Elden Pueblo. The style of most of these items closely resembles the simplified style of contemporaneous clay figurines from the Hohokam area.

after the Sunset Crater eruption was anything but random. Sites near Hohokam ball courts are 17 times more likely to have shell than sites away from ball courts, and cremations at Winona Village had larger amounts of shell as offerings than inhumations. Evidently, people did not adopt Hohokam-style ball courts in isolation—they were accompanied by a complex of behavior including the use of red-on-buff pottery, the manufacture and exchange of shell jewelry, and a cremation mortuary ritual.

Evidence for a Chacoan presence or influence in the Sierra Sin Agua is less abundant and more ambiguous than traces of the Hohokam connection. Nonetheless, some archaeologists believe that a few sites, such as Wupatki Pueblo and Ridge Ruin, served as late great houses on the far western frontier of the Chaco system.

The unique site of Ridge Ruin rests on a volcanic outcrop about two and a half miles east of Winona Village. A pueblo of 20 or more rooms overlooks two ball courts to the north. These prominent features are surrounded by a dispersed settlement consisting of clusters of pit houses and

associated trash mounds similar to those at Winona Village. Tree-ring dates indicate that the pit house village was inhabited between 1080 and 1130 ce, about the same time as Winona. The hilltop occupation began with some pit houses in the early 1100s and expanded with the construction of the pueblo beginning in the 1110s and continuing until after 1130. Datable pottery sherds found near the ball courts suggest that the courts were used at the same time as the pit houses.

At the core of the pueblo, people built the earliest 10 rooms with carefully prepared, evenly coursed slabs of sandstone rather than the more easily obtainable local basalt. Small pieces of sandstone decorate the mortar between the coursed masonry (see fig. 9.1). John McGregor, the archaeologist who directed the excavations at the site in the 1930s, remarked that "the most outstanding single feature is the close identity of the sandstone slab walls to those found in the Chaco Canyon Culture." Several later researchers have agreed with McGregor's assessment, suggesting that Ridge Ruin might be one of the westernmost of the Chacoan great houses.

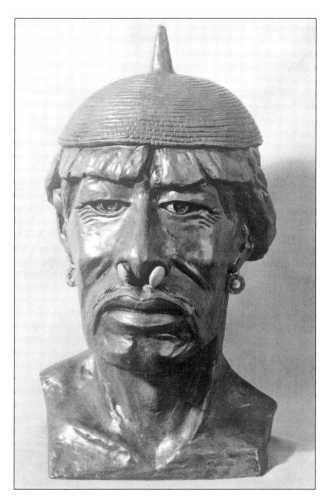

Figure 9.6. Artist's conception of the twelfth-century man known as the Magician, created in the late 1930s at the Museum of Northern Arizona. He is wearing a nose plug of the type shown in plate 28.

Although not nearly as "great" as the true Chaco Canyon great houses such as Pueblo Bonito and Chetro Ketl, Ridge Ruin is great in its local context. Like other Chacoan great houses, it lies at the center of a dispersed community. Ridge Ruin is distinguished by a series of terraced plazas, elevated spaces on which ceremonies could have been performed before the gathered populace. Similar terraced plazas appear at only two other sites in the Sierra Sin Agua: the nearby site of Two Kivas (perhaps founded by people who once lived at Ridge Ruin), and Citadel Pueblo in Wupatki National Monument.

Sometime in the 1170s the occupants of Ridge Ruin left their pueblo, just after the burial of an important man who has come to be known as the

Magician. Accompanying his burial, archaeologists found several sets of ritual paraphernalia, probably used in ceremonies intended for weather control, curing, male initiation, the countering of witchcraft, and warfare. The most spectacular items were a set of wooden swallowing sticks with carved handles that were either painted or encrusted in shell and turquoise mosaic. Ethnographers have documented how, among the Pueblo Indians and other Southwestern groups, priests swallowed specially decorated sticks in public demonstrations, to the amazement of onlookers. Just as modern performers do, they straightened the throat in line with the esophagus and then inserted the stick into the mouth and down the throat. Stick-swallowing ceremonies often had associations with weather control, the curing of throat ailments, and warfare. Some Zuni Indians said the ceremonies originated in Chaco Canyon.

Like Ridge Ruin, Wupatki contains a core of rooms with Chaco-style masonry and sits at the center of a dispersed community made up mostly of smaller sites. The multistory, compact, towerlike southern block of rooms at Wupatki is reminiscent of several Chacoan sites that rise high above the surrounding terrain. Wupatki's "amphitheater" might be an unroofed version of a Chacoan great kiva. Some rooms at Wupatki feature bands of basalt stones that contrast sharply with the more abundant red sandstone, a pattern of masonry also observed at some Chacoan sites. In addition, Wupatki has produced the remains of macaws, shell trumpets, and artifacts of polished jet (see fig. 19.5) —all items associated with Chacoan great houses but with few other sites of the time period. Some other sites in the Flagstaff area, such as Elden Pueblo, held carved bone and other artifacts resembling similar items from Chacoan sites.

On the frontiers of the Chaco and Hohokam systems, people of the Sierra Sin Agua experimented with architectural forms and cultural practices borrowed from their neighbors—such as ball courts, great houses, great kivas, and cremations—or developed locally, like the terraced plazas at Ridge Ruin. They adopted and adapted artifact styles and ritual artifacts that served as important symbols during a time of rapidly changing social relations in the late

Figure 9.7. A banded masonry wall at Wupatki Pueblo, an architectural style shared with some sites of the Chaco culture.

Figure 9.8. An ancient shell trumpet from Wupatki Pueblo (left), of the genus *Murex*, with a modern shell shown at right for comparison. Such trumpets are found at major sites of both the Chaco and Hohokam cultures.

1000s and early 1100s, after the eruption of Sunset Crater brought turmoil and opportunity. These events in the Sierra Sin Agua can be seen as a preview of the fourteenth-century gathering of the

Figure 9.9. A carved bone ornament (top) and decorated bone hairpins from Elden Pueblo. The ornament at top resembles items rendered in shell from the Hohokam culture area. The carved designs on the hairpins, especially the example at left, are reminiscent of pottery designs from Chaco Canyon.

clans at the present Hopi Mesas that is recounted in oral traditions. In these traditions, peoples of diverse backgrounds joined and contributed to one another's success through equitable cooperation. It may be that the Hisat'sinom were predisposed to accept diversity in the 1300s largely because they had already done so in the preceding centuries, in the shadow of Sunset Crater.

F. Michael O'Hara holds an M.A. in anthropology from Northern Arizona University. He has worked at the Museum of Northern Arizona, for several private environmental consulting companies, and with the Kaibab Vermilion Cliffs Heritage Alliance. At the time of this writing he is a doctoral student in anthropology at Arizona State University, working on a dissertation looking at cooperation and conflict during the post-eruption archaeological period in the Flagstaff area.

Figure 10.1. Examples of the three main pottery wares archaeologists have used to interpret the cultural affiliations of people in the Sierra Sin Agua. *From left*: Tusayan Gray Ware (Kayenta branch of the ancestral Pueblos), San Francisco Mountain Gray Ware (Cohonina), Alameda Brown Ware (Sinagua).

Peoples of the Sierra Sin Agua

Christian E. Downum and Daniel Garcia

Visitors and archaeologists alike have long wanted to know, "Who lived in the Sierra Sin Agua?" But identities are difficult to pin down, even for modern people. We humans express a sense of who we are according to many factors: gender, family relations, social status, social roles, occupation, language, cultural affiliation, geographical place, and history. For the ancient past, archaeologists can only try to infer from material remains the way people conceived of themselves, perceived their territories and boundaries, and related to others.

Still, people do use material culture to signal concepts of who they are. Archaeological clues such as house styles, pottery, clothing, and the remains of ceremonies such as funeral rites hint at individual and collective identities. So, too, does evidence of violent conflict—dramatic testimony about boundaries and group rivalries. In places like the Sierra Sin Agua, Native oral traditions often tell about the identities and movements of ancient peoples in and around known archaeological sites.

Archaeology in the Sierra Sin Agua began in the early 1900s with the idea that the farming peoples of the area had evolved in a typical "Puebloan" cultural sequence, from residence in stone-lined pit houses to life in above-ground pueblos. By the early 1930s, Southwestern archaeologists no longer viewed all ancient cultures as having built on a basic Puebloan pattern. They believed multiple cultural identities had once existed, each embodying a constellation of material traits that were

repeated among all archaeological sites of a particular "culture."

In 1932, for example, Emil Haury, at the Gila Pueblo Archaeological Foundation in Globe, Arizona, named the ancient irrigation farmers of Arizona's southern deserts "Hohokam," a Piman term for "exhausted" or "all used up." To Haury, the Hohokam, with their buff-colored pottery, shallow pit houses, ball courts, and cremation rituals, had a distinctive cultural identity far removed from that of the Puebloans and more closely aligned with peoples in what is now northern Mexico. At first this idea met with some resistance—one archaeologist referred to Haury's ideas as "Ho-hokum"—but archaeologists soon accepted the idea that ancient Southwestern peoples represented considerable cultural diversity.

In 1934 the founders of the Gila Pueblo Foundation, Harold and Winifred Gladwin, recognized several ancient cultural "roots," which later sprouted stems and branches, all representing geographically based cultural patterns distinctly removed from that of the Puebloans. They attempted to link contemporary language groups in the Southwest to the ancient cultures. The main roots they named were Puebloan, Hohokam, Yuman, and Caddoan, which Haury later changed to Mogollon.

Meanwhile, archaeologists working around Flagstaff were discovering archaeological remains that did not easily fit into the existing cultural categories. Many sites displayed unexpected combinations of pottery, architecture, and other characteristics then

Figure 10.2. *Left to right*: archaeologists Emil Haury, Arthur Hauck, and John McGregor, 1927. Haury went on to define the Hohokam and Mogollon cultural patterns in the Southwest, and McGregor was instrumental in defining the Sinagua culture.

Figure 10.3. Museum of Northern Arizona archaeologist Lyndon Hargrave, about 1930. In the late 1930s Hargrave and his colleagues at MNA defined the Cohonina archaeological culture.

Figure 10.4. Harold S. Colton, founder of the Museum of Northern Arizona. Photograph probably taken in the 1940s.

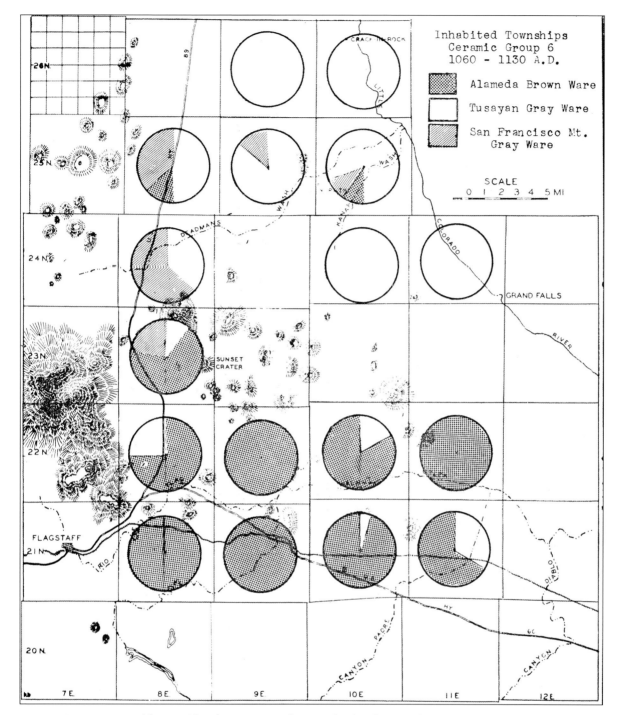

Figure 10.5. Map created by Harold Colton in 1946, showing the distribution of pottery wares in the form of pie charts for 17 six-by-six-mile townships.

considered typical of Hohokam, Mogollon, and Pueblo cultural roots. In 1933 Lyndon Hargrave, of the Museum of Northern Arizona (MNA), identified the "amphitheater" at Wupatki as a version of a Chacoan great kiva (see chapter 9). Two years later, MNA archaeologist John McGregor proposed that

about a dozen bowl-like depressions around Flagstaff were Hohokam-style ball courts. Tree-ring dates proved irrefutably that different kinds of arti- facts and architecture existed simultaneously only short distances apart.

On the basis of such evidence, Harold Colton,

director of the MNA, developed the view that the Sierra Sin Agua had once housed people from several cultural groups analogous to ethnographically described tribes. The groups could be recognized, he argued, on the basis of locally made, utilitarian pottery wares, each reflecting a group's sense of its cultural identity. As Colton recognized, pottery encodes the manufacturing choices and techniques that mothers passed down to their daughters over the generations. It says something about the intergenerational learning systems that formed an element of ancient cultural identities.

Colton believed archaeologists could identify the cultural territories of such "tribes" by plotting distributions of pottery wares. That is, they could calculate, for all the potsherds excavated from an archaeological site, the percentages made up of pieces of different wares, and then they could compare the percentages among many sites across the landscape. Colton did this for townships—areas measuring six by six miles—and presented the numbers in pie charts on a map. The results showed clear geographical differences in the proportions of three important pottery wares. In most areas, one ware predominated over the others.

Using these findings, Colton and his colleagues argued that before the eruption of Sunset Crater, culturally discrete populations lived in well-defined territories separated by natural barriers. Just northeast of the Flagstaff area lived groups representing the Kayenta branch of the Pueblo cultural root. Their utilitarian pottery—the vessels they used for daily cooking—was Tusayan Gray Ware. East and south of the San Francisco Peaks resided a group that Colton called the Sinagua. He was unsure of

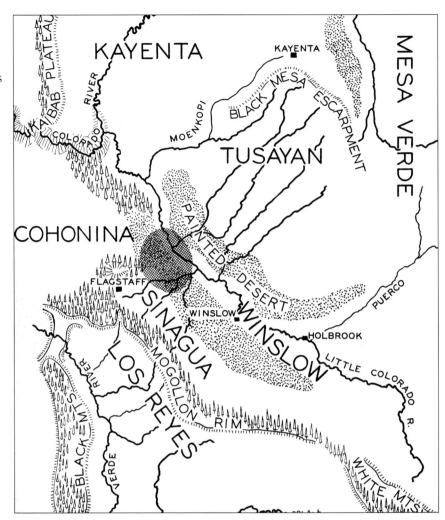

Figure 10.6. Map from Harold Colton's 1939 publication "Prehistoric Culture Units and Their Relationships in Northern Arizona," showing ancient cultures of northern Arizona and the natural barriers between them. Darkened area at center is the core of the Sierra Sin Agua.

its origins but tentatively assigned it to the Mogollon cultural root. Sinagua people made Alameda Brown Ware as their utilitarian pottery, crafting it from locally available volcanic clays in a curious mix of techniques for shaping and firing. A group that Lyndon Hargrave designated the Cohonina, assigned to the Patayan root, inhabited the forests and scrublands north and west of the San Francisco Peaks. The Cohonina made San Francisco Mountain Gray Ware pottery.

Colton identified cultural frontiers, 6 to 10 miles wide, that separated these branches. Drawing on his background as a zoologist, he colorfully described the frontiers as resembling "a semi-membrane on which the attributes of the branches are

Figure 10.7. MNA archaeologist Jimmy Kywanwytewa, about 1935.

MNA researchers believed that when Sunset Crater erupted in the late 1000s, it broke apart the cultural membranes along the frontier, and cultural identities in the area changed dramatically. Because the eruption opened up new farming opportunities, people from surrounding regions migrated into the "black sand" area of volcanic cinders. In this archaeological story, people with Hohokam, Pueblo, and Mogollon cultural identities all took up residence in the volcanic ash zone, bringing with them their respective pottery, architectural styles, and burial practices. Colton wrote that for several decades a "cosmopolitan" culture existed, although it eventually evolved into "a uniform Sinagua culture with pueblo architecture."

Although it was not explicitly recognized at the time, the MNA view of the Flagstaff area as a place of cultural mixing fitted well with Hopi oral traditions and might even have been influenced by them. Jimmy Kywanwytewa, a Hopi who excavated many archaeological sites for the museum, told MNA researchers stories about connections between Hopi clans and ancient sites along the eastern side of the San Francisco Peaks. He interpreted archaeological finds from a Hopi viewpoint, helping to strengthen the researchers' sense that Flagstaff-area sites had been home to Hopis. In one published account, titled simply "A True Story," Kywanwytewa related that Hopi ancestors had once buried a man at Wupatki pueblo with his "pets," a dog and some parrots. Archaeologists had in fact excavated such a burial at Wupatki. When the museum excavated the famed "Magician" burial at Ridge Ruin (chapter 9), some Hopi men, including Kywanwytewa, accurately predicted the full set of items that would be found with the bones. Edmund Nequatewa, another Hopi scholar at MNA, contributed additional stories of Hopi cultural connections with ancient ruins. These accounts probably influenced the MNA researchers of the 1930s to perceive an especially strong link between Flagstaff-area archaeology and the Hopi people.

In retrospect, Colton's characterization of the post-eruption cultures as "cosmopolitan" mirrors, in some ways, the Hopi concept of Hisat'sinom. In the Hopi view, the Hisat'sinom were not a single cultural or linguistic group but a mixture of peoples

beating like so many molecules in a liquid." Some cultural traits, such as pottery styles, passed through the frontier membranes easily. Others, "such as methods of manufacture of pottery, language, social structure, and religion," could not. Archaeological sites along the frontiers showed confusing mixtures of traits, Colton wrote, because they were places where "occupation fluctuated and cultures inter-mixed."

who had long ago split in their paths over the landscape. At some point, probably within the past several centuries, some of the clans and other offshoots of a larger Hisat'sinom population converged in the Flagstaff area, meeting up with a small group of local Motisinom who had never traveled far from their original homes. Under the urging of the Motisinom, the people then conceived of a new way of life known as the Hopi way, which rejected the complicated religious systems and competition that had previously existed. If one were to substitute the terms Hohokam, Mogollon, Sinagua, Cohonina, and Pueblo for the names of the migrating clans described by the Hopis, oral traditions and archaeology would not be fundamentally incompatible.

Today, archaeologists still use terms such as Kayenta, Sinagua, and Cohonina as a sort of archaeological shorthand, referring to sites where particular pottery wares predominate. But they no longer endorse the idea that such labels signify neatly bounded linguistic groups or political entities analogous to modern American Indian tribes or nations. Instead, the prevalent view is that the distribution of material traits across the landscape is a topic for investigation, not an assumed reality of cultural identity. Contemporary researchers want to know how specific groups of people, at a particular time and place, lived and interacted with others around them.

Other ideas, too, have changed since the 1930s. Research by Peter Pilles, Paul Fish, and Suzanne Fish, for example, has largely discredited the notion that Hohokam and Mogollon people immigrated into the Sierra Sin Agua en masse after the eruption of Sunset Crater. The constellation of Hohokam-like features and artifacts at some post-eruption sites seems to represent a much smaller movement of people than Colton envisioned. Pilles is also skeptical that the eruption had far-reaching effects on patterns of settlement in the Sierra Sin Agua. He points out that during the early 1100s, people across large parts of northern and central Arizona were moving from higher to lower elevations anyway, probably for reasons related to climate. Only sometimes, he believes, did they coincidentally move into places directly affected by the ash fall.

Recently, we revisited the topic of pottery distributions as possible markers of ancient cultural

identities in the Sierra Sin Agua. Enjoying a vastly larger archaeological database than researchers had at their disposal in the 1930s, we looked at data from more than 16,000 sites scattered from the Mogollon Rim north to the Grand Canyon and from the western edge of the Coconino Plateau to the Hopi Mesas. Our goal, like Harold Colton's, was to see whether pottery distributions—and therefore, potentially, cultural identities—varied geographically, with significant boundaries. Our findings largely confirmed the earlier conclusions reached by MNA archaeologists, but with a new twist having to do with places where violent conflict broke out.

Using geographic information systems (GIS) computer software, we created a series of maps plotting the percentages of the three major kinds of utility pottery—Alameda Brown Ware, San Francisco Mountain Gray Ware, and Tusayan Gray Ware—at sites across the Sierra Sin Agua. We depicted the pottery percentages as if they were topographic peaks and valleys on a three-dimensional contour map.

We found that before the eruption of Sunset Crater, peaks of Alameda Brown Ware, San Francisco Mountain Gray Ware, and Tusayan Gray Ware indeed tended to coincide with the traditionally defined territories of the Sinagua, Cohonina, and Kayenta branches, respectively. Our maps also showed gaps, or buffer zones, between pottery concentrations. After the eruption, the contours of the pottery percentages become ragged toward the edges of the ceramically defined territories, with isolated peaks for individual wares. We believe this reflects a spatial mosaic of cultural identities along the frontier zones, much as Colton and his MNA associates intuited from sparser information in the 1930s.

Plotting the boundaries of pottery distributions for the immediate post-eruption years, from about 1080 to 1140 CE, we found a startling relationship between those boundaries and Flagstaff-area sites showing evidence of violence. Archaeologists have known for years that sites in and just south of Wupatki National Monument contain intentionally damaged human remains, burned houses, and other traces of ancient conflict. One well-known case is the "House of Tragedy," a small pueblo and pit house site excavated by MNA archaeologist Watson Smith in the late 1940s. There, a young man and

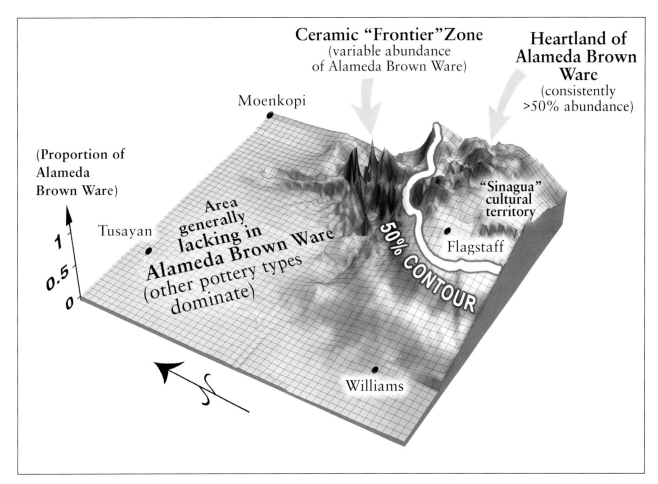

Figure 10.8. Three-dimensional contour map of percentages of Alameda Brown Ware at sites in the Sierra Sin Agua, 1080 to 1140 CE. Each percentage is shown as if it were the elevation of a ground surface. The separate "peaks" north of Flagstaff may represent isolated Sinagua settlements in a frontier zone following the Sunset Crater eruption.

woman had evidently been killed and their remains mutilated and scattered across the floor of a pit structure. Nearby sites showed scattered human remains on the floor of a burned pit house and isolated cases of human bones having been burned and cracked open. Jack Smith Alcove House, a burned pit structure near Sunset Crater, contained only the torso of a man with a set of arrow points near his ribs.

These cases were recently supplemented through excavations by the consulting firm Desert Archaeology during an expansion of U.S. Highway 89. The Deadmans Edge site was particularly revealing. There, five people whose remains lay on the floor of a burned pit house were, as excavators Deborah Swartz and Mark Elson put it, "clearly not typical burials." Two were adult women, and the other three were children and young adults from ages 11 to 17. Their bodies had been twisted into unusual positions, and some of them were partly stuffed into subfloor pits. The skull of one person had been smashed, and it appeared that the oldest woman had been bound. According to the excavators, the house had burned down onto these remains just around the time of death. Charred posts and beams lay directly on human bones.

We found a striking correlation between the locations of these sites and a ceramic frontier winding between concentrations of Alameda Brown Ware, San Francisco Mountain Gray Ware, and Tusayan Gray Ware. All but one of the known sites with evidence of violence lay in and along this frontier zone, where no one ceramic ware predominated. When we examined the tree-ring and ceramic dates from the sites, we received another

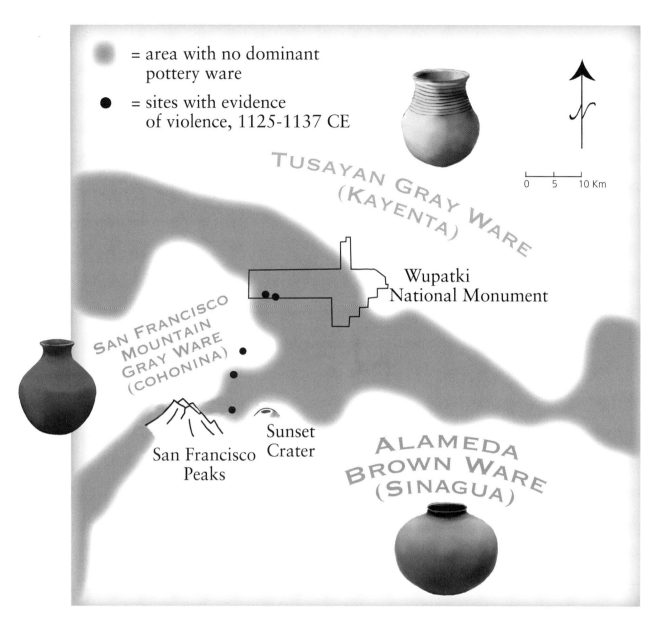

= area with no dominant pottery ware

= sites with evidence of violence, 1125-1137 CE

0   5   10 Km

TUSAYAN GRAY WARE (KAYENTA)

Wupatki National Monument

SAN FRANCISCO MOUNTAIN GRAY WARE (COHONINA)

San Francisco Peaks

Sunset Crater

ALAMEDA BROWN WARE (SINAGUA)

Figure 10.9. Locations of sites dating from about 1080 to 1140 CE that show evidence of violent conflict. They lie along a frontier zone (shown in gray) where no one pottery ware predominates. Areas with sites containing 50 percent or more of Tusayan Gray Ware, San Francisco Mountain Gray Ware, or Alameda Brown Ware are shown in white.

surprise. All of them fit within the 13 years from 1125 through 1137.

The correlation of violence with a ceramically defined frontier suggests that such acts had their roots in cultural conflicts. In the early 1100s, as people colonized the Wupatki area after the fall of the Sunset Crater ash, people of different identities encountered one another daily for the first time. Disputes over rights to use the land might occasionally have escalated into violence. When the worst

drought of the twelfth century struck in the 1130s, control of farming territory must have become more crucial than ever. Differences in cultural identities might have exacerbated an already trying set of circumstances. Indeed, Hopi oral traditions tell of a time in the Wupatki area "when people couldn't get along," and violence erupted. But the post-eruption conflicts appear, like the volcano itself, to have flared briefly and then subsided, perhaps as groups learned to accommodate one another or as some groups became more powerful and consolidated their territories.

The science writer Steve Olson, referring in his book *Mapping Human History* to treelike diagrams of human genetic relationships, wrote that "such trees are fundamentally misleading because they do not show the links among groups. Human groups are more like clouds forming, merging, and dissipating on a hot summer day." In the long human history of the Sierra Sin Agua, many "clouds" of cultural identity surely appeared and disappeared. We have only begun to discern their outlines.

Daniel Garcia is an archaeologist, a geographic information analyst, and the assistant director of the Cultural Resource Group at EcoPlan Associates, Inc., an environmental consulting firm in Mesa, Arizona. He holds a master's degree in anthropology from Northern Arizona University and has conducted field and research projects in the greater Flagstaff area since 2000.

Figure 11.1. Aerial view of Wupatki Pueblo with its ball court (foreground) and "amphitheater" (the circular unroofed structure)

Wupatki Pueblo

Red House in Black Sand

Christian E. Downum, Ellen Brennan, and James P. Holmlund

The Wupatki Basin makes a picturesque but seemingly improbable spot for a major center of Hisat'sinom life. Towering cliffs of black basalt rim a red sandstone desert where soil lies thin atop bedrock, trees are stunted and sparse, and even drought-adapted shrubs and grasses struggle to survive. Hot and dry for much of the summer, the basin averages a little over eight inches of precipitation a year—less than the quintessential desert city of Tucson, Arizona. In winter, fierce blizzards can drop more than a foot of snow and plunge the temperature to below zero. Springtime brings howling winds to whip up clouds of reddish brown dust and rearrange the thick, rippled dunes of black volcanic cinders.

Yet in this unlikely setting, the walls of Wupatki Pueblo began to rise nearly 900 years ago. Within about three generations it grew into a four-story, 100-room structure and became the heart of a thriving pueblo community. At Wupatki's peak in the late 1100s, it stood as the region's largest and tallest pueblo—surely a cultural center for people of the surrounding region. It likely served as a gathering place, a trading center, a treasury of exotic goods, a landmark, and a place for sacred rituals and ceremonies.

The name Wupatki can refer not only to the pueblo but also to Wupatki National Monument, the Wupatki Basin, the Wupatki Archaeological District (a property on the National Register of

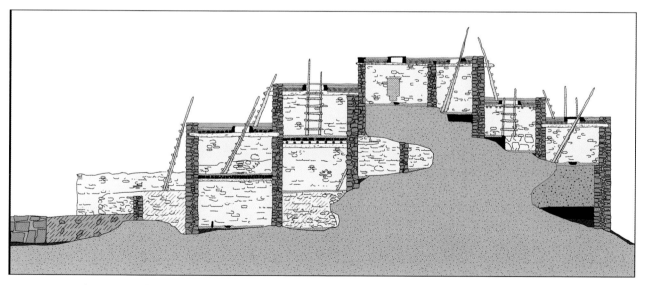

Figure 11.2. Schematic profile of the south room block of Wupatki Pueblo, reconstructed from archaeological evidence gained during excavations in 1933 and 1934.

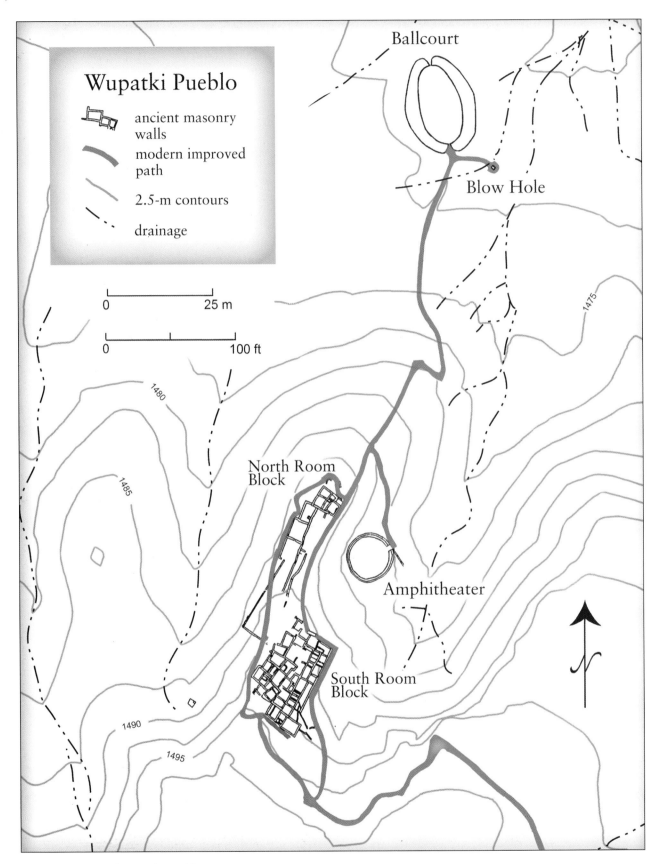

Figure 11.3. Plan of Wupatki Pueblo.

Figure 11.4. Aerial view of the north and south room blocks at Wupatki.

Historic Places), and the ancient pottery type Wupatki Black-on-white. The word has traditionally been thought to derive from the Hopi name Wupakikuh, "Tall House Ruins." Wupatki Pueblo received that name officially, probably at the suggestion of archaeologist Harold Colton, when President Calvin Coolidge set aside land in 1924 to create Wupatki National Monument. Another Hopi name for Wupatki, preferred by some Hopi elders and scholars, is Nuva'ovi, or "Place of the Snows."

Wupatki Pueblo emerged in the early 1100s, a time when great Southwestern cultural traditions that had endured for centuries were changing rapidly. To the east, the people living in Chaco Canyon, their influence waning, had mostly stopped building their "great house" pueblos and kivas. To the south, an important phase in the Hohokam way of life was also drawing to a close. Hohokam people, who had for so long expressed their worldview and religion through games played in ball courts and fiery death rites involving cremation, were just starting a "Classic" period that repudiated such things.

Closer to home, residents of the Colorado Plateau were rearranging themselves on the landscape. From the late 1000s through the 1130s, an enigmatic group of Hisatsinom known to archaeologists as the Cohonina left their homeland west of the San Francisco Peaks and moved eastward onto the pine- and juniper-clad mesas just south of Wupatki. Around 1140, Hopi ancestors known archaeologically as Kayenta Puebloans began retreating from distant outposts and concentrating in a much smaller territory east and north of the Little Colorado River. After the Sunset Crater eruption, many so-called Sinagua people relocated from the ponderosa pine forests around modern Flagstaff to lower-elevation grasslands to the north and east. At the time of these movements, people in the region were living in small, widely spaced hamlets and villages of scattered pit houses and modest, one-story pueblos.

Only a few decades before Wupatki began to grow, the Sunset Crater volcano had belched its final clouds of steam, leaving the landscape utterly altered. Area farmers, who previously had written Wupatki off as too hot and dry for cultivating, took note of the thin blanket of cinders covering the earth downwind and downslope from the volcano. This "black sand" was having a beneficial mulching effect and enabling trees, shrubs, and grasses to thrive. Even if the Wupatki Basin still wasn't a great place to farm, it might now be among the least bad during bad times. The stage was set for a population boom.

Like many other ancient pueblos, Wupatki developed on the remains of earlier structures. Unfortunately, we know little about them; the evidence consists only of thin deposits of artifacts under rock overhangs, masses of charcoal representing burned and collapsed rooms or pit structures, and a few storage pits.

Once people started to build the pueblo of Wupatki, it grew irregularly. Builders added rooms as they were needed, not aiming for consistency in size, shape, construction techniques, or internal features. Generally, the pueblo grew outward and upward from a core of early rooms placed against and atop the bedrock at the southern end of the village and from a nucleus of rooms built around large boulders at the north end. Eventually, builders joined the north and south room blocks into a single, continuous structure. Interestingly, the earliest rooms at Wupatki display what some researchers have interpreted as a Chacoan style of masonry, with carefully shaped and arranged stones. The roughly hewn, irregularly stacked masonry of the later rooms better resembles that of nearby Puebloan structures to the north and east.

Archaeologists are fortunate to have a large number of tree-ring samples with which to date Wupatki Pueblo. We estimate that the pueblo's builders cut at least 1,670 pieces of wood for roof beams, upright posts, and doorway lintels. Of these, 183 survived to provide tree-ring dates, 90 of them "cutting" dates—that is, the precise year when a tree died, usually because someone cut it down. Nearly half this wood came from Douglas fir and spruce trees that Wupatki's builders could have found only near the San Francisco Peaks, some 12 to 20 miles south of Wupatki.

Tree rings tell us that the first wood-cutting episode took place in the mid- to late 1130s. Additional clusters of dates then appear every 7 to 15 years, perhaps as families grew or immigrants

Figure 11.5. View into the Wupatki ball court from its narrow northern entrance.

moved in. After 1200 construction diminished, and by about 1215 Wupatki's residents seem to have stopped building new rooms. A few tree-ring dates from the mid-1200s appear after a gap of a few decades, marking a later reoccupation of the pueblo or perhaps a handful of stubbornly persistent families who had hung on all along.

Probably early during the construction, Wupatki's builders added two large, unroofed ceremonial structures, likely for performances that were accessible to most or all of the pueblo's residents. One, sited about 400 feet beyond the north end of the pueblo, is an oval depression lined with stone masonry and measuring about 45 by 90 feet, with narrow doorways at each end. It so resembles Hohokam ball courts that archaeologists have named it the Wupatki ball court. We believe this structure, along with about 12 similar courts throughout the Sierra Sin Agua, once hosted a game in which players used a rubber ball imported from

Mexico. Some Hopis disagree, believing it more likely served as a dance court, perhaps for rituals involving the Snake clan.

The other ceremonial structure is a carefully made, circular, stone-walled enclosure just east of the pueblo. Known to archaeologists as the Wupatki amphitheater, the building measures about 45 feet in diameter and has an encircling bench. It vaguely resembles Chaco-style great kivas or, more accurately, some of the large, kivalike structures built in the northern Southwest after most people had departed Chaco Canyon. We do not know exactly when the ball court and the amphitheater were built; neither has produced a tree-ring date. Judging from pottery, both seem to have been used throughout the life of the pueblo.

Another great open-air construction was a large, rectangular plaza built along the west side of the pueblo, now mostly collapsed and eroded. The plaza's builders first erected an impressive retaining wall, in some places up to eight feet high, and then filled the area behind it with stones, trash, and soil. The resulting platform served as a place where people could gather, socialize, work, and perform public ceremonies. Another possible plaza lies along the east side of the pueblo, surrounding the amphitheater. Such large, open-air plazas are rare at twelfth-century pueblos in the region. The two examples at Wupatki, along with the amphitheater and ball court, suggest that this pueblo became an important meeting place, with no contemporary equal nearby.

Adjacent to the ball court sits an impressive geological feature known as a "blow hole," one of many in the area. At the surface, blow holes look simply like small cracks or holes in the bedrock, but they lead deep underground to a massive set of interconnected, natural rock chambers. Depending on atmospheric pressure, a blow hole either expels or inhales air at a high velocity. On a hot summer day, cool, musty air rushes out of the Wupatki blow hole with great speed and force. In winter, wind from the blow hole feels relatively warm against the cold surrounding air.

Ancient people might have interpreted blow holes as meaningful links between the underworld, the surface world, and the sky. Modern Pueblo people commemorate the connection between surface and subsurface worlds with the *sipapu*, a small hole in the floor of a kiva. To the Hopis this feature symbolizes the original place of emergence, the Sipapuni, where the first humans entered this world by climbing up from the underworld.

The people of Wupatki probably came from many places at different times. In archaeological terms, the "cultural affiliation" of Wupatki's residents remains a puzzle. Anthropologists have conducted few detailed studies of burials at Wupatki, but the little information that exists portrays a diverse population. Some people had flattened skulls, a slight deformity caused by harmless pressure exerted by cradles on the growing skull bones of infants. This pattern was common among Sinagua people to the south. But several people buried at Wupatki had undeformed skulls. Some people were placed in the grave in a "flexed" position, with the body tightly folded; others were laid out fully extended. At the time, flexed burials were

common among people mostly to the north, and extended burials were more frequent in the south. Wupatki has even yielded one cremation burial, a practice usually associated with the Hohokam.

Architecture and artifacts tell a similarly complex story. Architectural styles at Wupatki show both Chacoan influence and, later, similarity to nearby Kayenta pueblos. The pueblo's ball court and an abundance of shell jewelry suggest that its people also had some affiliation with Hohokam people—or perhaps Hohokam ideas—from far to the south. Much of the pottery excavated at Wupatki originated in the vicinity of modern Flagstaff, but a substantial portion came from the Kayenta country to the north. Remnants of cotton cloth show styles and decorative techniques found in several parts of the Southwest (see chapter 18).

Consistent with these archaeological findings, Hopi and Zuni oral traditions portray Wupatki as a place where people of diverse origins lived briefly on their way to their ultimate stopping points, villages on the Hopi Mesas in Arizona and in the vicinity of modern Zuni Pueblo in northwestern New Mexico. The Havasupais, who now live along the south side of the Grand Canyon, have their own oral traditions linking them to Wupatki. Navajo people, too, hold strong ties with the Wupatki area, having lived there since at least the early 1800s.

Archaeologists have debated over Wupatki for more than a century, ever since the Smithsonian Institution's Jesse Walter Fewkes interviewed Hopis in the 1890s and early 1900s, trying to piece together the routes Hopi clans had followed during their migrations toward the Hopi Mesas. In the 1990s David Wilcox, of the Museum of Northern Arizona, interpreted Wupatki as an outgrowth of the Chaco cultural system. To Wilcox, Wupatki was a regional political and trade "nexus," strategically situated between desert scrublands and pine forests, connecting peoples to the south with the Kayenta world to the north and the Chacoan world to the east. Wupatki, a local form of a Chacoan great house, arose because of the ambitions of people who traded—literally—on the mystique of Chaco Canyon.

More recently, Glenn Stone and Chris Downum proposed that Wupatki indeed grew because of its

Figure 11.6. Museum of Northern Arizona archaeologists excavating Wupatki Pueblo in the early 1930s.

role in political processes, but those processes were largely local. In this explanation, intense competition over farmland in a risky agricultural environment led to violent conflicts among groups of different cultural origins (see chapter 10). Some groups organized themselves along ethnic lines to protect and expand their landholdings. Pueblos such as Wupatki, the Citadel, and other large, visually prominent communities served as symbolic expressions of political power as well as central places in local political, religious, and economic life.

In the view of some Hopi scholars, Wupatki came into existence and fulfilled its destiny as intended by spiritual forces. In this view, no more needs to be asked of the pueblo, and no scientific explanation is required. Its true meaning is to be found in its place in Hopi cultural history and its significance to Hopi people.

Tree-ring evidence shows that by the mid-1200s,

Wupatki Pueblo lay empty. Whatever sparked the exodus, it surely was wrenching. The pueblo represented an enormous investment of human labor, emotion, and hope. The departure, though, seems to have been orderly. Unlike many other ancient Southwestern pueblos, especially those of later time periods, Wupatki was not burned. We think the intact roofs, sealed doorways, and many valuable things left in the rooms imply that at least some people expected to return someday.

Why did they decide to leave? A severe drought between 1215 and 1221 correlates neatly with the cessation of building. Studies of plant remains from pack rat nests built up over many years in Wupatki National Monument indicate that by the early 1200s the area had been largely denuded of trees and shrubs, which people needed to heat their homes and cook food. Farmers had cultivated nearly every possible location that could have been planted, and with repeated use, the fields lost nutrients vital for sustaining crops. Perhaps new pueblos, new communities, and new opportunities promised more than Wupatki could offer to its younger and more restless residents. Internal dissension or threats from neighbors, as well as prophesies or other beliefs, might also have influenced decisions to leave.

For a brief time after Wupatki fell silent, life there survived in the memories of people who had resided in or visited the great place. Eventually, those memories passed away, too. Wupatki Pueblo receded into legend, becoming part of the stories elders told as they recounted the many places where their ancestors had lived and the adventures they had experienced while walking the tangled paths of ancient migrations. Today, under the care of the U.S.

National Park Service, Wupatki enables the footprints of the present to mingle with those of the past in the fine red dust of ancient floors.

Ellen Brennan is the cultural resource program manager for Grand Canyon National Park. She holds a master's degree from Northern Arizona University, and her interests include ceramic chronologies, architecture, and Grand Canyon archaeology.

James P. Holmlund, president of Western Mapping Company, in Tucson, Arizona, has created hundreds of precise maps of ancient pueblo and pit house sites in the Southwest, including the first high-precision GPS map of Wupatki Pueblo. Recently he pioneered the use of three-dimensional lidar scanning for documenting artifacts, architecture, and rock art.

Figure 12.1. Hopi mother and child, photographed around 1900.

Children of the Sierra Sin Agua

twelve

Kathryn Kamp

Imagine the sounds of a Sierra Sin Agua village. Fires crackle softly. A dog barks. Footsteps pass, some heavy and slow, some firm and purposeful, others rapid and light, running through the village. A baby cries. Voices—male and female, old and young—speak, sing, laugh. Children whisper secrets, shout happily, or cry with anger or frustration.

Archaeologists long ignored age and gender when they studied ancient people, because those attributes leave few material traces. By the 1980s, researchers had begun to think about gender roles. Today, although they still seldom discuss the elderly, they are paying more attention to children.

The people of the Sierra Sin Agua left no pictures of their offspring or written accounts of their lives. The few unambiguous traces of children include their graves, child-size sandals, and occasional small handprints. Along with the scant direct evidence, archaeologists rely on cross-cultural patterns of childhood worldwide and draw analogies from historical accounts of Hopi and other Puebloan groups.

As in nonindustrial societies everywhere, the ancient inhabitants of the Sierra Sin Agua were mostly young. Adults seldom lived as long as they do in modern, industrially developed countries. People in their forties and fifties would have been elders, and many people died before they reached such ages. About half the burials excavators have found in the Sierra Sin Agua are those of children. Infant and early childhood mortality was high. Weaning was a time of stress, and mothers probably postponed it for several years to help protect their children.

Teeth and bones can reveal much about the conditions in which people lived. Illness and poor

Figure 12.2. Hopi child looking out a small window in a pueblo, around 1900.

nutrition leave lines called enamel hypoplasias on teeth, evidence of the slowing or temporary cessation of enamel formation. Scientists can determine a person's age at the time of the stress by examining the location of the hypoplasia on the tooth. Similarly, in long bones such as the tibia, a bone of the lower leg, any temporary slowing of growth causes what researchers call Harris lines. From studies showing enamel hypoplasias and Harris lines in children of the Sierra Sin Agua, it is clear that they struggled with disease and periodic food shortages.

Children who survived infancy probably began to work very early. Until recently, most children around the world played important economic roles, working on farms, in factories, or in small craft production. In ancient and historic Pueblo societies, children's work and play typically were closely related, and both taught vital adult skills. As they watched adults and participated in household activities, children learned the social and technological skills and the moral values they needed to become successful

Figure 12.3. Hopi children helping with the replastering of pueblo walls, about 1900.

adult members of society. Cross-culturally, this pattern of education is more common than are formal lessons or schooling.

Clara Naranjo, of Santa Clara Pueblo, described children's work as she knew it in her 1992 Ph.D. dissertation, "Social Change and Pottery-Making at Santa Clara Pueblo": "One of the things that children incorporated very early into their consciousness was that work was necessary to feel good about oneself and to have others think well of you. If it was said that you were a 'hard worker' you felt you were paid one of the highest compliments.... As

children, we carried our younger brothers and sisters on our backs while we swept the plaza area, helped get clay or mixed the clay with temper. We also mixed the mud with our feet for making adobe and mortar. After the mud was mixed, we also helped carry the bricks and mortar to build the walls. Cooking was done by girls from a fairly young age. Boys were off in the fields helping with hoeing, harvesting and in the mountains hunting and fishing."

Even very young Sierra Sin Agua children most likely ran errands, helped clean the house, and

Figure 12.4. Miniature pots from Elden Pueblo, probably made by children in the twelfth or thirteenth century.

cared for even younger children. Cross-culturally, the most common task for children under the age of six is collecting wood for fuel. We have no concrete archaeological evidence that Sierra Sin Agua children did so, but families certainly needed wood daily to maintain fires in household hearths for cooking and heating.

Water was another constant need, especially since few villages in the Sierra Sin Agua sat near water sources. In more than 90 percent of nonindustrial societies, children fetch water. Among some historic Pueblo peoples, they began doing so as early as four years of age, using small containers that they could carry. Archaeologists have not yet tried studying the sizes of broken jars found near water sources or on trails leading to them, in order to understand the role ancient children played in this task.

As parents collected medicinal herbs and edible plants to supplement the crops they grew, their children learned by helping them. Children helped with farming, too. Even the youngest could chase away birds and rodents that threatened the crops. Because good fields in the region tended to be small and scattered, the people of the Sierra Sin Agua often built temporary shelters near their farm plots during the growing season. Some household members, perhaps elders and children, lived in these field houses so that they could easily take care of daily weeding, pest removal, and watering. Children might even have helped by doing things like piling snow on the fields in winter, to increase soil moisture in the spring when the snow melted.

Cross-culturally, the work assigned to young children tends to be repetitive and time consuming and to require no intense concentration. It may involve tasks done by either men or women. As children grow older, their responsibilities shift toward those customary for their gender. In the Sierra Sin Agua, older girls would have spent considerable

Figure 12.5. Clay figurines from Lizard Man Village. Many such figurines show child-size fingerprints, suggesting they were made by children.

time grinding corn and cooking. Historically, Hopi girls started grinding corn at about age eight, and adult women spent several hours a day performing this essential task. Girls also learned to sew and make pottery and baskets.

For boys, becoming an adult meant learning to hunt, make stone tools, use weapons, and farm. Information about historic Pueblo peoples suggests that boys also learned to weave cotton cloth and make stone and shell jewelry. Both boys and girls had to gain appropriate ceremonial and religious knowledge as they grew up.

Little evidence so far reveals much about how Sierra Sin Agua children learned crafts, but fingerprints left in ancient clay provide some clues, at least for pottery making. They also reveal something about prehistoric play. I came across these fingerprints—and found my interest in the children of the Sierra Sin Agua piqued—when I studied

artifacts from Lizard Man Village, a site I excavated with my husband, John Whittaker, and several field schools of Grinnell College students.

At this hamlet of pit houses and later pueblo rooms, we found 78 small clay figurines, mostly depicting four-legged animals, perhaps dogs. They tended to be crudely made, and most of them had been broken before being discarded in the trash. We found two damaged but fairly whole figurines, however, in the grave of an adolescent. Some previous investigators had suggested that such figurines were ceremonial; others thought they were toys. When we examined the figurines under a hand magnifying lens, we saw that some of them bore partial fingerprints—traces, perhaps, of the ages of their manufacturers.

I eagerly searched for information about ways to determine age from partial fingerprints, but I found little. John even tried calling the FBI, assuming that

Figure 12.6. Close-up of adult-size fingerprints on Tusayan Corrugated pottery, about 1050 to 1250 CE.

its agents knew more about fingerprint identification than anyone else. An FBI representative claimed to have nothing to offer but asked that we share our results if we found a useful method. Some existing research did suggest that a measurement called ridge width might be worth investigating. Ridge width is the width of a single ridge and its adjacent valley in a fingerprint. As people grow and their hands become larger, ridge widths increase.

In order to discover the precise relationship between ridge width and age, my students and I took fingerprints from a sample of adults and children of varying ages, tapping connections at local day care centers, schools, and scout troops. We had each person in the sample make a clay figurine similar to those we had found at Lizard Man Village. Correlating ridge widths of partial fingerprints in the clay with those of their known makers, we found that we could indeed use ridge width measurements to assess age.

The ancient fingerprints from Lizard Man Village showed that people from the ages of four years to adulthood had made the figurines. Apparently, Sierra Sin Agua children were playing and practicing with clay while still very young. The fact that the figurines had been fired told us that grownup potters had helped the youngsters. The resulting toys thus combined play and learning.

Another source of fingerprints came in the form of locally made pottery decorated with a technique called corrugation. The potter coiled the basic form and then pinched the coils to produce a textured surface. When I looked at fingerprints on pieces of large, well-made corrugated pots, I found that the majority were adult size, but some vessels appeared to have been made by children as young as 10. By engaging young children with clay, adults encouraged them to develop a sensitivity to the medium, the kind of familiarity that enables learners to become competent relatively early.

Figure 12.7. Hopi children playing in pool of rainwater at Oraibi Pueblo, about 1900.

It comes as no surprise, of course, that Sierra Sin Agua children played; children do everywhere. But unlike making clay figurines, many kinds of play leave little or no identifiable evidence. For example, Hopi girls historically used the foot bones of sheep to make dolls, but in an archaeological site, bone dolls are just bones unless they have been altered to look more like dolls or have been placed in girls' burials as offerings. Similarly, items that children borrowed from adults, as well as natural objects such as sticks, stones, feathers, and seeds that they used without modification, are invisible as toys to the researcher. Preservation is another issue; toys made of wood, cloth, or other perishables rarely survive.

Archaeologists have found game pieces—flat, shaped pieces of bone or pottery—in Sierra Sin Agua villages, but they do not know exactly how ancient people used them. Adults as well as children like to play games, and historically, gambling was not uncommon among Southwestern Indians, so we cannot directly link such tokens to children. A ceramic disk found at Medicine Cave, just west of Sunset Crater, had a knotted buckskin thong about eight inches long strung through a hole and knotted again on the other side, suggesting that the disk was used as a whirligig. But was it adults or children who used such artifacts? There is no way to know.

In the many small Sierra Sin Agua villages, home to only one or two extended families, children might have had few age mates to play with. They must have played with children both older and younger and perhaps were closely integrated into adult activities. In larger communities, children of similar ages might have had the chance to play together, apart from adults. In either case, the friendships children created probably influenced future alliances between family groups.

Dramatic changes in the way people housed and fed themselves took place in the Sierra Sin Agua between about 1050 and 1300 CE. Some of those changes must have altered children's diets and therefore their health. The kinds of tasks children performed might have changed, as did the number and kinds of people they grew up with and even the safety of venturing far from home. As children grew to young adulthood, they might have challenged their elders to adopt new customs and let old traditions slide. In this regard, as in many other facets of the lives of Sierra Sin Agua children, we must interpret the archaeological evidence using both ethnographic information and creativity.

Kathryn Kamp, Earl D. Strong Professor of Social Studies in the anthropology department at Grinnell College, has worked in Arizona, Belize, Syria, Jordan, and Turkey. Her interests include prehistoric childhoods, experimental archaeology and ethnoarchaeology, and adaptation and social complexity in the American Southwest.

Figure 13.1. A Hopi field house, about 1885.

Farmsteads and Field Houses
The Big View from Small Sites in Wupatki National Monument

Jeanne Stevens Schofer

On a typical June afternoon, visitors to Wupatki National Monument are struck by a paradox. How did this hot, bone dry, seemingly inhospitable landscape host a thriving population of farmers in the eleventh and twelfth centuries? In some places, more than 100 archaeological sites per square mile pack the monument. Ancient pueblos seem to dot every mesa top.

Why did people choose to live here, and how did they survive? Important clues come from the smallest archaeological sites in the monument, the kinds of humble dwellings that researchers often overlook in favor of more dramatic subject matter. Among them are the ubiquitous field houses—small, often single-room structures used mostly as shelters for farmers in their fields. Thousands of them stood in the vicinity of Wupatki Pueblo between 1050 and 1250 CE, making up more than half of all ancient sites in the area. The farming strategies of Pueblo peoples in historic times

tell us much about the way the Hisat'sinom of the Sierra Sin Agua must have used their field houses and other, somewhat more permanent small structures.

Historically, Pueblo farmers cultivated fields in more than one location, to help insure themselves against the risk of crop failure in any one place. If the distance to a field was short, family members usually walked there to work for the day. When a

Figure 13.2. Remains of a field house near Wupatki National Monument. The stones once formed a low wall, above which builders fashioned a post-supported brush roof and perhaps brush or jacal upper walls.

plot lay a little too far from home for a day's round-trip walk, people built simple shelters where family members stayed for a few days or weeks at a time while tending the field. Using brush, rock, wood, jacal (brush reinforced with grass and mud), or some combination of these materials, they might erect no more than a lean-to or a ramada, a roofed area without enclosing walls. Sometimes they built small houses—enclosed spaces with doorways. These informal, temporary structures are usually what archaeologists have in mind when they talk about field houses.

In 1900 Cosmos Mindeleff, an archaeologist with the Bureau of American Ethnology, described the movement of Hopi people among outlying farming settlements as "continuous." Similarly, in the 1930s the anthropologist Elsie Clews Parsons described the movement between pueblos and farming outposts in New Mexico as "constant traffic." Besides serving as temporary living quarters, such structures helped mark land claims, signifying that a particular family was cultivating a given area.

Sometimes Pueblo people traveled a little farther to outlying fields and built more substantial houses nearby, where they stayed all summer. Historically, many continuously occupied pueblos grew out of such simple farmsteads. Examples are the Zuni settlements of Black Rock and Nutria, New Mexico, both of which were once clusters of farm houses used only during the growing season. Laguna Pueblo in New Mexico originated as a farming outpost established by some families living at Acoma Pueblo. At Isleta Pueblo, along the Rio Grande, three farming hamlets started as simple, seasonal outposts.

To learn more about how people used small

Figure 13.3. A Hopi brush lean-to used as a temporary shelter for farmers, about 1885.

sites in the Sierra Sin Agua during the time of great change after the Sunset Crater eruption, I analyzed all the 463 known architectural sites in Wupatki National Monument that dated from about 1068 to 1160 CE. Predictably, the most abundant kind of site, making up 57 percent of the whole sample, was the field house—a small structure made mostly of ephemeral materials. Field house sites, as I defined them, had few stone structures, no pit house depressions, and few artifacts, with no chipped or ground stone tools. These sites gave every indication that their makers had built them quickly and used them briefly for only occasional household chores.

The next most numerous kind of small site, at

Figure 13.4. A Zuni farmstead in the 1880s.

37 percent of the sample, was what I called a farmstead. This was a somewhat larger, more substantial structure than a field house, with a slightly greater number and variety of artifacts (although still not many). Farmsteads usually had several rooms, and people probably lived in them all summer. Generally, they yielded few potsherds, but they had surprisingly large numbers of chipped stone tools such as knives and arrowheads. Perhaps people used farmsteads as hunting camps, too. Historically, Hopi men are known to have hunted antelope in the Wupatki area during the winters. Earlier people might have done the same, using their summer farmsteads as base camps.

A third kind of small site I looked for was what I called permanent habitations. Although they made up only 6 percent of all sites of the early post-eruption period, permanent habitations had many rooms and often included one or more pit houses. They also contained abundant, diverse artifacts, including pieces of broken cooking and serving pots; stone slabs and hand stones (manos and metates) for grinding corn and grass seeds; chipped stone tools such as arrow points and knives; and hammer stones and debris from the manufacture of stone tools. These were places where people lived year-round, engaging in all the daily tasks households typically carried out.

All 463 sites stood near some kind of water catchment feature—usually a small, seasonal reservoir made by building a low earth and rock berm across a small drainage or by excavating soil and rock from a shallow depression in bedrock. Catchments for collecting melted snow and rainwater are plentiful in the Wupatki area, for obvious reasons. They do not hold water for long after a rain or snowfall, so the water that collected in them had to be quickly transferred to large water jars for storage. Most of the sites, indeed, produced potsherds from black-on-white, decorated pottery jars used to transport and store water. A few displayed fragments of ladles used to scoop water from catchment to jar. Sites near reservoirs had many more sherds from decorated pottery jars than other sites had. Apparently, settlers who moved into the Wupatki area after the volcanic eruption solved the problem of getting drinking water by constructing small, seasonal catchments and situating their field houses, farmsteads, and dwelling sites within reasonable walking distances of them.

Figure 13.5. Ancient reservoirs at Wupatki National Monument, dating between about 1070 and 1220 CE. *Top:* a reservoir during the dry season. *Bottom:* a reservoir filled with water during the summer rainy season.

Figure 13.6. A Dogoszhi Black-on-white jar and a Holbrook Black-on-white ladle, both dating to about 1050–1200 CE. Pottery vessels like these were essential for collecting and storing water from ancient reservoirs.

Clearly, after the eruption people built many small shelters and other structures as they explored the landscape and tried to figure out where they could farm and live successfully. The scarcity of permanent habitation sites demonstrates that few people yet chose to make permanent homes here. Even so, the overall rate of site construction is impressive. Between the eruption of Sunset Crater and 1160 CE, settlers on average built a structure or left a scatter of artifacts that lasted to become an archaeological site about every 25 days. They built field houses, farmsteads, and small pueblo or pit house settlements at the rate of about one every two months. The turnover rate was equally remarkable. People seem to have used most of these sites only briefly, presumably then moving on to a more promising place.

But who were the people who chose to come to Wupatki? Where did they come from? How did their lifeways and patterns of settlement vary? To answer these questions, I collected additional information from a sample of 17 early post-eruption sites.

Like Harold Colton and other researchers before me (see chapter 10), I found that the pottery from these sites usually fit into one of four categories: mostly San Francisco Mountain Gray Ware, the pottery made by "Cohonina" people west of the San Francisco Peaks; mostly Tusayan Gray Ware, made by ancestral Puebloan people who lived in a large area of northern Arizona centered on the modern town of Kayenta; mostly Alameda Brown Ware, made by "Sinagua" people living around modern Flagstaff, Arizona; and a mixture showing no dominance of any one pottery ware.

Sorting the sample according to these ceramic groups, I could see that the Cohonina sites, with San Francisco Mountain Gray Ware, had larger, better-built structures containing relatively diverse artifacts. Several of them appeared to have been permanent habitations. Sites with more Tusayan Gray Ware (Kayenta sites) displayed smaller, less elaborate structures and fewer, less diverse artifacts. Most of these sites were field houses. The Sinagua and ceramically mixed sites were diverse, including field houses, pit houses that might have been permanently occupied, and a rock shelter.

Geographically, Cohonina sites clustered in the western part of Wupatki National Monument. Kayenta sites lay widely dispersed across a plain known as Antelope Prairie (see map 4). The early Sinagua and mixed sites tended to be concentrated in the central portion of the monument, especially in the vicinity of what would later become Wupatki Pueblo.

In short, although the people archaeologists now call Cohonina, Kayenta, and Sinagua lived similar lifestyles, they appear to have settled the Wupatki landscape very differently after Sunset Crater erupted. Cohonina families likely moved in from the south and west of today's Wupatki National Monument, establishing a relatively small number of continuously occupied settlements within a few miles of a homeland that reached as far north as the middle Deadman Wash.

People who used mostly Sinagua pottery originated to the south of the monument, in the ponderosa pine forest surrounding modern Flagstaff. Some of these colonists might have been displaced by the volcano. They settled in the vicinity of Wupatki Pueblo and seem not to have moved far beyond that area.

For Kayenta people who colonized Antelope Prairie in the late 1000s and early 1100s, home was an area north of the Little Colorado River, an important physiographic feature that seems also to have been a persistent cultural boundary. Field houses in the Wupatki area were among the first structures Kayenta groups built south of the river. Droughts that hit in the 1090s and the 1130s might have spurred families to explore new farm sites in the cinder-mulched land across the Little Colorado.

Small details in the sites also reveal cultural differences. Cohonina and Sinagua sites yielded consistently fewer decorated pottery vessels than sites associated with Kayenta people, who are known for their beautifully painted black-on-white bowls and jars. Cohonina farmers showed a definite tendency to orient their settlements toward the southeast, whereas the Kayenta and Sinagua groups more often oriented theirs toward the northeast. Such variations among groups hint at differences in beliefs and behavior at which we can only guess.

The large picture painted by small sites in Wupatki National Monument portrays people of at least three cultural identities settling on newly productive farmland after the Sunset Crater eruption. Some families seem to have explored the area experimentally at first. They put up temporary field houses or small farmsteads and cultivated a few plots for a season or two before deciding to live in the area year-round. Others came to stay permanently, committing from the beginning to make this wide-open landscape their home. Consistent with Hopi oral traditions, this place near the San Francisco Peaks might well have been home, for a time, to people who saw themselves as clans meeting up in their travels over the landscape.

Jeanne Stevens Schofer, the North Zone archaeologist on the Gila National Forest in west-central New Mexico, holds an M.A. in anthropology from Northern Arizona University. She has also worked as an interpretive park ranger and archaeologist for the National Park Service in northern Arizona and as an archaeologist for the U.S. Forest Service in east-central Arizona.

Figure 14.1. Traditional Hopi pueblo architecture: the village of Shungopavi at night, about 1900.

Ancient Architecture in the Sierra Sin Agua

Lloyd Masayumptewa

My name in the Hopi language is Piivayouma. In the *pahaana* (modern American) world, I am Lloyd Masayumptewa. I am a Hopi from the village of Orayvi (Old Oraibi). Although by Hopi tradition I should claim my mother's village of Munqapi (Moenkopi) as my home, I was raised by my paternal grandparents in Orayvi. I grew up in a stone pueblo similar to the ones archaeologists now study in the homeland of my ancestors, the area surrounding Nuvatukya'ovi, the San Francisco Peaks. My boyhood home was a two-story house with rooms each made of a single thickness of mud-mortared, hand-shaped sandstone blocks. The ceiling and roof consisted of layers of wooden beams, split pieces of juniper, bundles of brush, and, on top, clay soil.

When I was young, it seemed as if home repairs were never-ending, if we wanted a warm, dry place to live. The summer rainy season threatened our traditional architecture the most. I remember that when the roof started to leak, my grandfather would get some mud and go out in the pouring rain to patch it. When the rain stopped, the rest of the family would make necessary repairs, such as re-mudding the walls, resetting stone, and inserting small stones to chink holes and cracks in the walls.

Today, I still help repair pueblos, but in a different capacity. I now work as an archaeologist and ruins preservation specialist for the U.S. National Park Service (NPS). Much of my job involves helping to preserve the Hopi ancestral homes that stand in national parks and monuments around Flagstaff, Arizona.

Hopi people refer to ancient houses of the Sierra Sin Agua as *hisatsinmuy qii'am*, or "homes of people from long ago." We know little about the earliest

Figure 14.2. Lloyd Masayumptewa (*right*) at work in Wupatki Pueblo.

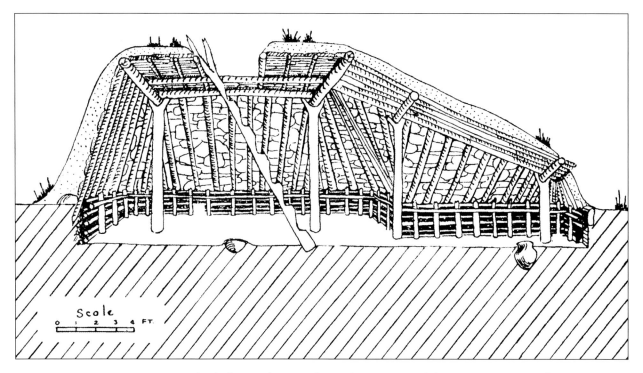

Figure 14.3. Artist's reconstruction of a shallow pit house with an "alcove," situated about two miles west of Sunset Crater.

houses in the region, because the Motisinom, the nomadic people who hunted and gathered there before farming arrived (see chapter 8), built no permanent structures. Their seasonal homes were simply brush huts or other perishable shelters that left few traces for archaeologists to find.

The earliest permanent dwellings were pit houses—excavations of various sizes, shapes, and depths, roofed with wood beams, brush, twigs, grass, and mud. The floors of shallow pit houses might lie just a few inches below ground. Such dwellings often had thin walls made of small poles interwoven with branches and plastered with mud. Useful during the warmer seasons, they were poorly insulated for winter. People often entered them through ground-level entryways, sometimes covered under a small vestibule.

Other pit houses reached depths of six feet or more, which probably insulated them well against winter cold at high elevations. Deep pit houses had heavy roofs supported by large upright posts, usually four of them placed in a square just inside the pit walls. People went in and out of the deeper pit houses through a large hole in the roof, which could be covered by a mat, an animal skin, or a flat stone. A thick, notched log, placed so that it sloped down to the floor, gave access into and out of the roof opening. In one pit house archaeologists found the burned remnant of such a log embedded at an angle in the floor. Deep pit houses received air through a ventilator, a cleverly constructed shaft, sometimes lined with stone or wood, that ran from floor level to the ground surface outside the house. Fresh air entered the house through this shaft and then passed out through the roof opening, taking smoke and stale air with it.

Inside a pit house, people commonly scooped out a shallow, circular hole in the floor and lined it with a thin coat of clay, creating a hearth for heating and cooking. Sometimes they dug pits beneath the floor in which they stored foodstuffs such as shelled corn and grass seeds.

Pit houses evolved over time. In the area east and south of the San Francisco Peaks, for example, the earliest pit houses, starting about 550 CE, were large, circular, and relatively shallow—roughly 30 inches deep—with long, covered entryways. Sloping post holes around the perimeters suggest that these houses once had walls forming a conical, tepee-like structure. Later, from about 825 to 1090 CE, people

Figure 14.4. Artist's reconstruction of a deep pit house in the Sierra Sin Agua, based on evidence from archaeological excavations. The opening at the base of the right-hand wall is one end of the ventilator shaft, which opens at ground surface farther to the right.

H.S.C
1931

dug deep pit houses and sometimes lined them with upright posts or split planks of pine. These helped keep the earthen walls of the pit from slumping and might also have helped insulate the house against the cold, damp ground.

The transformations on the landscape wrought by the Sunset Crater eruption brought changes in local architecture as well. House styles evolved and diversified rapidly between about 1090 and 1140 (plates 11, 12). Tree-ring dates show that houses of many different sizes, shapes, depths, and internal features existed simultaneously, only a few yards from one another in a single village. At Winona Village at least one house, overlooking a ball court, was a Hohokam-style pit house. The site's excavators also believed that some houses there showed influences from people far to the southeast, whom archaeologists call Mogollon.

Some builders now lined their deep pit houses with carefully laid stone masonry. These houses

resembled later above-ground pueblos, except that the stone walls lined a pit rather than standing above the ground surface. After the mid-1100s the Hisat'sinom began to curtail their construction of pit houses. They lined most of the few they did build with stone masonry, and archaeologists believe these rooms served mainly as places for ceremonies rather than as living quarters.

A few above-ground rooms had existed in the Sierra Sin Agua as early as the 800s. As pit house living waned after the mid-1100s, pueblo-style architecture grew widespread. Most pueblos were small—just a few single-story rooms, usually facing east or southeast (plates 4–5, 13, 14). Often, such dwellings appear in clusters, loosely grouped into small communities. Among the rarer large, multi-story pueblos were those now called Wupatki, Elden, Turkey Hill, Wukoki, and Citadel Pueblos.

Across the Sierra Sin Agua, pueblos can be seen made of sandstone, basalt, limestone, dacite (a type

Figure 14.5. Wukoki, a multistory pueblo at Wupatki National Monument dating between about 1140 and 1220 CE.

of light-colored volcanic stone), and combinations of these—whatever the builders found close at hand. Most of them had roofs of ponderosa pine or fir beams, sometimes carried in from forests many miles away. In a few cases, low walls extended outward from the structure itself, delimiting a partially enclosed plaza. Sometimes people built pueblo rooms inside natural rock alcoves; the ruins of some of these can still be seen in Walnut Canyon National Monument.

The Walnut Canyon cliff dwellings and imposing Wupatki Pueblo—the two major pueblos of the Sierra Sin Agua that can now be visited by the public—illustrate the area's diverse building styles. At Wupatki, people built rooms either by stacking stones on top of each other in a single row or by

building up parallel walls a few inches apart and filling the hollow interiors with irregular stones and gravel. The latter method made sturdy, well-insulated walls that could support upper stories. In either case, the builders needed little mortar and no chinking stones, because they used sandstone that came naturally in flat, tabular slabs that required little shaping. These they could easily pick up from the ground surface or peel off from bedrock outcrops. When complete, interior walls received a layer of white or gray plaster. Outside walls remained unplastered.

Few ground-level rooms at Wupatki had entryways. Instead, residents entered them by climbing up one ladder to the roof and down another from a hatch in the ceiling. Upper-story rooms had entryways

Figure 14.6. Pueblo rooms constructed around 1200 CE in a natural alcove at Walnut Canyon.

penetrating their exterior walls and were often connected to other rooms through interior entryways.

For their roofs, the builders of Wupatki started by felling locally available trees such as junipers, ponderosa pines, aspens, and small cottonwoods with stone axes. The trunks or thicker branches became the major roof beams, to be covered first with brush or reeds, then with a layer of a grassy material, and finally with clayey dirt. The grass helped keep the dirt from filtering down into the room. Dirt with a high clay content not only shed rainwater better than silty soil but also was heavier, so it would not blow off readily in a high wind.

At Walnut Canyon, too, the Hisat'sinom used what Mother Earth provided nearby. There the rock consisted of irregular blocks of limestone, which, unlike the sandstone at Wupatki, required builders to use plenty of mud mortar and many chinking and leveling stones to make walls stable. They were spared from having to cut trees to roof their alcove

rooms, because the natural rock ceilings served as roofs.

Rooms at Walnut Canyon tend to be unusually large, and each had a wide, rectangular door that opened toward the canyon bottom. Some entryways led from raised platforms, or "porches," placed just outside the room entrance, so that people had to step down to enter the room. Adjacent rooms are rarely connected by entryways, which researchers interpret as meaning that each room was an all-purpose dwelling for a single family. Alcoves provided excellent shelter, and people used nearly all available space in them for their homes.

Like the Puebloan peoples of the Colorado Plateau, the Hisat'sinom of the Sierra Sin Agua seem to have carried out rituals and ceremonies in special rooms now called kivas. Some kivas were small and either circular or rectangular in plan. Large, circular, unroofed "great kivas" resembled structures known by that term in Chaco Canyon, New Mexico. Other

Figure 14.7. An excavated example of an ancient community room in the Coconino National Forest.

special places included oval, unroofed structures similar to the Hohokam ball courts of the southern Arizona desert and very large, rectangular rooms that local archaeologists call "community rooms." Certain pueblos feature walled, cleared plazas that closely resemble the plazas of modern Hopi pueblos, where ceremonies still take place today. What archaeologists have called "forts" in the Sierra Sin Agua—large structures built at the tops of volcanoes and ridges (plate 7)—might have served as ceremonial gathering places, too, although in fact their uses remain unknown. They might also have served as defensive refuges in times of conflict (see chapter 20).

Nature eventually reduces ancient pueblos to mounds of stone and earth. In the meantime, preservation specialists with the National Park Service and other agencies battle the forces that threaten to bring these ancient buildings down—natural erosion, the weakening of walls by previous excavations, the consequences of public visitation,

and simple gravity. Today, documenting the ruins to create a permanent record of them for the future is viewed as an important form of preservation. At NPS we use a variety of high-tech tools to document architecture: mapping, aerial photography, high-resolution digital photography, and three-dimensional laser scanning. If a site collapses or is otherwise damaged or destroyed, we have a record of what existed.

Modern preservationists also consider "backfilling," or reburying excavated sites under dirt, an important tool. When archaeologists dig sites, they expose ancient walls and interior features to gravity and erosion. Only continual maintenance keeps such structures standing, and even then, important features can be quickly lost once they are exposed to the elements. Too little funding is available to stabilize all the exposed sites in the Southwest, so for many pueblos, backfilling is by far the best overall means of preservation.

Sometimes, preservation methods themselves

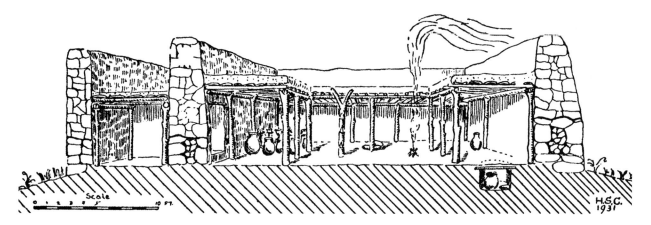

Figure 14.8. Artist's reconstruction of Medicine Fort, a large, hilltop structure about three miles west of Sunset Crater.

can be the culprits behind new problems in ruins stabilization. One of the worst decisions ever made by early preservationists was to use Portland cement as a mortar to hold old stone walls together. Not only is cement unsightly and incompatible with the natural materials used by early builders, but it actually proved to be destructive to the soft stone and mud mortar used in Southwestern pueblos. Today, architectural preservation specialists have returned to the same materials the original builders used. Although we sometimes add glues or hardeners to our mortars, it is only because we still have not found the secret formula for making natural mud mortar last in the open air.

The only place I have seen that shows how things might have been done properly from the beginning is a site in Walnut Canyon that was reconstructed in the 1930s under the auspices of the Museum of Northern Arizona. Several Hopi men did the work, using what the original builders used and following as closely as possible the construction techniques of ancient times.

Many traditional Hopis do not like seeing our ancestral homes opened to the public and subjected to constant visitation. What I do to preserve ancient architecture and keep it open to the public goes against their wishes. I do it so that our young people can see places that, I hope, will convey to them how deep our history runs in the Southwest and how difficult life could be in the ancient past. By preserving ancient structures, we ensure that future generations can learn from and appreciate the lives and achievements of people of long ago.

Lloyd Masayumptewa holds an M.A. in anthropology from Northern Arizona University. He served as a project leader for the ruins preservation and archaeology program at the Flagstaff Area National Monuments (Wupatki, Sunset Crater, and Walnut Canyon) before becoming Chief of Cultural Resources at the Southern Four Corners Group (Navajo and Canyon de Chelly National Monuments, and Hubbell Trading Post National Historic Site). He is of the Water-Coyote clan, and his paternal clan is the Rabbit-Tobacco clan.

Figure 15.1. Evidence of farming from archaeological sites in the Sierra Sin Agua dating to around 1070–1300 CE. *From top:* tabular basalt hoes from Elden and Turkey Hill Pueblos; corncobs from Walnut Canyon; clay jar stoppers from Wupatki and Nalakihu Pueblos, showing impressions of maize and beans; partial wooden digging sticks from Wupatki.

House and Garden
Learning about Small Structures through Excavation

Ruth E. Lambert

The concept of "field houses"—small structures presumed to have been used for agricultural purposes—is one of the oldest ideas in Flagstaff-area archaeology. As early as 1918 Harold Colton identified such remains as the keys to understanding ancient farming peoples of the American Southwest. Archaeologists knew something about field houses in the Sierra Sin Agua from surveying ruined walls and artifacts on the ground surface, but what more might be learned from excavating these little sites? To find out, in 2000 I began the first relatively large project at Wupatki National Monument to look specifically at small structures rather than at bigger pueblos.

To make the project manageable, I zeroed in on the area surrounding a prominent pueblo known as the Citadel, the second largest archaeological site in the monument after Wupatki Pueblo. Built and lived in during the late 1100s and early 1200s CE, at roughly the same time as Wupatki, the Citadel formed the center of a thriving community. Throughout the surrounding area lie hundreds of small sites—everything from 20-room pueblos to single-room stone structures and traces of agricultural fields, terraces, rock alignments, water catchments, and check dams.

As a first step, I chose a sample of small sites representing the full range of variation in that part of the monument. After screening all relevant sites in the study area that were known

Figure 15.2. View of multistory, 50-room Citadel Pueblo, atop its small basalt mesa, looking west across the remains of Nalakihu Pueblo.

Figure 15.3. Archaeologists inspect a small farmstead site, dating to about 1140–1220 CE, on Antelope Prairie east of the Citadel.

from earlier archaeological surveys, I narrowed the sample down to 172 that appeared to be candidates for excavation. Of these, I visited 72, recording information about surface remains, and then excavated portions of 16 structures at 8 sites. I also dug small portions of several trash heaps and agricultural fields.

In excavating the sites, I paid careful attention to the subtle layering of sediments and cultural materials within structures. I collected artifacts and samples of soil containing ancient pollen and plant remains from precisely controlled levels. I carefully examined the geological composition of the deposits I unearthed and the pottery in them, in order to date the sites accurately.

Some of the findings from the excavations confirmed previous understandings of small sites, but surprises arose, too. One confirmation was that people had lived in the Citadel area for centuries, perhaps as early as the Archaic period. At one place, people had stayed in rock shelters intermittently over many years. The lowest excavated levels in these shelters contained abundant stone flakes left over from the chipping of tools such as projectile points and drills, perhaps left there by ancient hunters who camped in the caves. At least three levels in the rock shelters lay beneath deposits of Sunset Crater cinders. Evidently, long before the volcano erupted, bands of Hisat'sinom or even

Motisinom set up seasonal hunting and gathering camps at places like these.

Over time, people's use of small sites seems to have become progressively more oriented toward agriculture. Several garden areas dating relatively late in pre-eruption times suggested that farming was by then in full swing. Farmers' forays into the area were in the vanguard of later, post-eruption colonization by members of several cultural groups (see chapter 13).

Researchers had long supposed that ancient farmers used field houses and other small structures only briefly as they shifted their fields from place to place. My excavations corroborated this belief but added some nuances. Not only were archaeological remains scarce at all the studied sites, showing that no one had lived in them for long, but often the layers containing cultural remains were separated from one another by layers of naturally deposited dirt. In other words, some field houses had been used briefly but repeatedly, mostly over periods of less than 100 years, judging from pottery.

The pollen and plant remains I collected revealed much about what ancient people in the Citadel area ate. Corn pollen and charred kernels, cupules, and other parts of the plant came from floors, hearths, and ash pits in living structures. Clearly, people had once stored, prepared, and consumed maize at the sites. Maize pollen was also

Figure 15.4. An isolated small pueblo on Antelope Prairie just east of the Citadel. This structure, consisting of no more than a few masonry rooms, is typical of settlements in the last half of the 1100s.

present in many soil samples taken from farming terraces, from the soil built up behind rock alignments, and from other small growing areas. Pollen from squash, beans, and tobacco, found in structures and storage pits, demonstrated that people grew those domesticated plants as well.

Charred seeds and fragments of wild plants found in structures, storage pits, and gardens told their own story about the tremendous variety in long-ago diets. These Hisat'sinom ate, among other plant foods, piñon nuts, amaranth seeds, goosefoot (*Chenopodium*), tomatillo, purslane, beeweed, the greens and seeds of saltbush, and the flowers or young pads of cholla, prickly pear, and hedgehog cacti. Most of these plants could have been gathered in the near vicinity of the sites, and they, too, were stored, perhaps as insurance against crop failure.

One surprise was the discovery of seeds from domesticated cotton plants. Cotton demands a great deal of water, so I had hardly expected to find it in the Citadel area. Nonetheless, both cotton pollen

and seeds appeared in sediments taken from ancient garden plots. Perhaps people had laboriously carried water to the plants in pottery jars, or perhaps they were able to channel runoff from summer thunderstorms directly into their gardens. Other cotton seeds came from the dirt fill inside rooms and storage pits, implying that people had stored the seeds and possibly processed and ate them at these small sites.

The discovery of piñon nuts in several small structures was almost equally unexpected, because piñon trees do not grow in the immediate Citadel area. The closest groves lie dozens of miles away, in the woodlands north of the San Francisco Peaks and south of the Grand Canyon. Perhaps Hisat'sinom farmers ranged into such areas to collect these highly nutritious nuts in the fall, or perhaps they exchanged foods with people living nearer to the piñon woodlands. A regional system of food circulation might have helped people colonize places where agriculture was risky.

Fig. 15.5. Reconstruction of a small, seasonally used field structure in Wupatki National Monument, dating to around 1090 CE. Details are based on archaeological excavations conducted by Ruth Lambert in 2000. One side of the entryway and one wall have been omitted so that the interior is visible; in reality the structure was fully enclosed.

The pollen and plant remains established that 13 of the 16 excavated small structures were related to farming. A few sites in the area had been full-time habitations, but most consisted of shelters where farmers lived temporarily while planting, tilling, and harvesting their fields. Several other rock constructions—those without structural walls, roofs, or internal features, for example—served as garden plots, water catchments, and storage places. Near the few large, full-time residences, people often built terrace gardens. Soil samples from such terraces produced high counts of pollen and remains of domesticated plants.

Over time, the uses of individual small structures sometimes changed. Sites that originally served as camps for hunting and gathering bands became seasonally occupied farming outposts. Later, outposts might become shelters used only during the day, or they might be abandoned and never reused. Some day-use structures were eventually converted into uninhabited gardens, alongside original gardens that persisted throughout the years.

Besides revealing details of the way Hisat'sinom farmers lived their daily lives, the excavation of small structures in the Citadel area indicated that larger changes had taken place in land use patterns. Before the eruption of Sunset Crater, farmers in the region resided seasonally in dispersed farmsteads next to or near their fields. After the rain of volcanic cinders in the late 1000s, people began to live in larger pueblos and make day trips to work in their outlying fields and gardens. The former seasonal field houses either were converted into day-use structures or fell into disuse.

If the excavation of this small sample of 16 structures tells us so much about early life at Wupatki, then future excavation at other small sites across the Sierra Sin Agua holds great promise.

Archaeologist **Ruth E. Lambert** has worked in the Southwest for more than 25 years. She holds a Ph.D. in anthropology from the University of New Mexico. Currently, as cultural program director for the San Juan Mountains Association in Durango, Colorado, she works with volunteers to preserve archaeological and historical resources.

Figure 16.1. Ancient agricultural rock alignment on the CO Bar Ranch, just north of Wupatki National Monument.

Hisat'sinom Farmers and Their Fields

Gregory B. Brown

In the mid-1990s I worked as part of an archaeological crew surveying ruins on the CO Bar Ranch, a vast, windswept grassland about 15 miles northeast of the San Francisco Peaks. As our team walked the landscape, recording familiar archaeological remains such as pueblos, pit houses, and artifact scatters, we also saw many long lines of stones, usually spaced about three to six feet apart. Sometimes the lines seemed to be associated with the ruins of ancient houses, and many of them clustered in dense concentrations.

In three square miles of territory on the CO Bar Ranch, we documented 693 such lines of stone, collectively measuring 16,417 linear feet, or a little more than three miles. These results were consistent with findings from a previous survey of Wupatki National Monument, just south of the ranch, where archaeologists had discovered more than 12,000 rock lines spread across 55 square miles.

Curious, I wanted to learn more about these obviously man-made rows of stones. How old were they? What had the Hisat'sinom used them for? Traditionally, archaeologists working in the region referred to such features as "rock alignments," a term that plainly summarizes their appearance but tells nothing about why ancient people built them. Researchers tended to assume that these alignments either retained or funneled runoff from summer thunderstorms onto agricultural fields or helped protect young crops from the strong winds that blow in the Sierra Sin Agua in the late spring and early summer. But so far, rock alignments had attracted few rigorous studies.

Over the course of two years, I followed up on our survey by investigating the rock alignments of the CO Bar Ranch. I gathered precise data on their lengths, orientations, and spacing. I collected soil and pollen samples from the ground adjacent to the rows; probed nearby soil to measure its depth, composition, and ability to hold moisture; and made similar observations in areas lacking alignments. Finally, I excavated part of a small field house, one of many ancient structures associated with the alignments.

Analysis of pollen left little doubt that the alignments had something to do with farming. Although it is extremely difficult to obtain the pollen of crops grown in ancient fields, because they produce so much less of it than nearby, profusely pollinating wild species, I managed to recover maize (corn) pollen from two of the seven rock alignment sites I sampled. I also found clumps of pollen from edible plants such as goosefoot (*Chenopodium*) and amaranth, which suggested either that people intentionally grew such plants or that the plants flourished naturally in the disturbed soil of cultivated fields. I found no similar pollen clumps in soil samples from areas lacking alignments. Interestingly, the samples also yielded pollen from beeweed (*Cleome*), an edible plant that does not grow on the CO Bar Ranch today.

Examining the compass orientations of the rock alignments, I concluded that archaeologists had

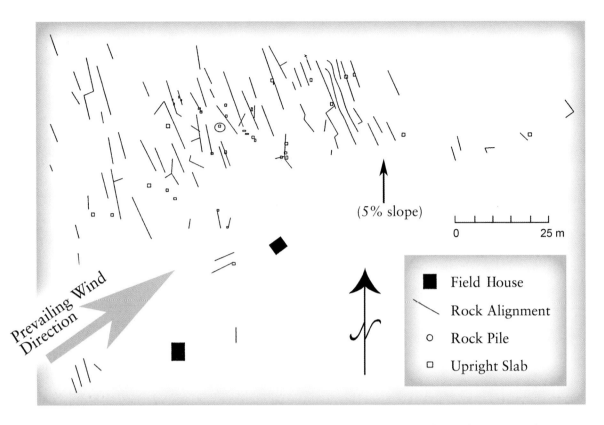

Figure 16.2. Map of a rock alignment field system on the CO Bar Ranch. Note the northwest-to-southeast orientation of nearly all the alignments, perpendicular to the prevailing wind direction.

almost certainly hit the mark in seeing them as windbreaks. The prevailing wind on the CO Bar Ranch, as in the entire region, comes from the southwest. That is, the wind nearly always blows toward a compass bearing of about 45 degrees, the point midway between north and east on a compass. The overwhelming majority of the measured alignments on the ranch, I discovered, stretched from northwest to southeast, perpendicular to the prevailing wind direction. On average, the alignments pointed toward 137 degrees on the compass —almost precisely southeast—and three-quarters of them were oriented toward a compass bearing between 130 and 170 degrees. Most of the rows that did not follow this orientation were very short segments placed perpendicular to longer alignments, as if to subdivide larger fields. The average rock alignment, then, lay within 2 degrees of a perfect 90-degree rotation from the prevailing wind, and the great majority deviated no more than a few degrees from this pattern.

This "against the prevailing wind" orientation of rock alignments held true regardless of the slope of the ground surface. For example, at one site with a gentle slope of 5 percent, the average orientation of 103 alignments was toward a compass bearing of 132 degrees. Another site, with 17 alignments on a steeper slope of 10 percent, showed an average orientation of 130 degrees. In neither case were the rock alignments oriented perpendicular to the slope, as would be expected if they functioned to slow erosion. Evidently, when people built rock alignments on the CO Bar Ranch, they were much more concerned with blocking the wind than with slowing or channeling the flow of runoff from thunderstorms.

These findings were at first a little surprising. In many other parts of the Southwest, ancient people often used rock alignments to control soil erosion caused by the flow of water and to hold back surface runoff long enough to allow the water to percolate into the soil. In the Wupatki area, though, soil erosion is not a big problem. Abundant rocks below ground and volcanic cinders on the surface help hold the soil in place. Here, in flat, mostly treeless terrain like that of the CO Bar Ranch, wind abrasion and the drying of young plants is the major problem to be solved. Using rock alignments mainly as windbreaks makes sense.

In the spring, the wind blows consistently at 30, 40, or even 50 miles an hour, with little to slow it down. Its effects on young shoots of corn are devastating. Not only does the wind buffet the young plants and dry them out, but it also sandblasts them with particles of sand and volcanic cinders. Especially after the eruption of Sunset Crater in the late 1000s CE, cinders blowing along the ground at high speed would have been deadly to newly sprouted corn. I believe the rock alignments on the CO Bar Ranch once consisted of stones placed upright in the ground, standing to heights of about a foot and shielding young maize planted on the downwind side. Because the alignments also retained runoff and kept the soil behind them relatively moist, they might have supported clumps of rabbit brush or other shrubs that helped to further slow and baffle the wind.

Several modern studies bear out the wisdom of ancient farmers in using rock windbreaks. From experiments involving a variety of crops, researchers have learned that yields can increase by an average of 14 percent when windbreaks are used. Although the most obvious effect of a windbreak is to reduce wind velocity, it can also shelter the soil from wind erosion; protect crop roots; modify temperature, humidity, evaporation, and solar radiation; increase snow retention; and generally improve soil moisture. Windbreaks create complex microenvironments that have effects far beyond merely slowing the wind.

The measurements I took on the alignments revealed that 84 percent of them were relatively short, between about 3 and 30 feet long. But I found two very long alignments, stretching for 230 and 500 feet, respectively. Arranged in an L shape, these two enclosed a set of smaller alignments. From these it appears that ancient farmers sometimes carefully delineated an area under cultivation, perhaps to let other people know they were

claiming the right to use a particular piece of land.

I also measured the overall sizes of fields containing rock alignments on the CO Bar Ranch. They varied a great deal, from about 650 to 200,000 square feet. Altogether, they covered roughly 2.7 million square feet, or about 3 percent of the total area surveyed.

How many people would these fields have fed? Using figures derived from the yields of historic Pueblo Indian fields, I calculated that the total quantity of maize grown in the three-square-mile survey area could have supported 31 to 57 people for one year. The average field could have fed one person for 4 to 7.5 months, and the largest fields would have supported two to four persons for a year.

An important concept in studying ancient farming systems is that of agricultural "intensification." In the 1960s, the Danish agricultural economist Ester Boserup proposed that humans often adjust their farming methods to cope with increasing population size. One common way they do so is to work harder per unit of land, making improvements to fields in order to increase agricultural yields.

Do the rock alignments at the CO Bar Ranch represent a case of agricultural intensification? Probably not. The fields marked by alignments there are unimpressive in comparison with other ancient Southwestern field complexes. For example, archaeologist Linda Cordell studied a gridded field system in the Rio Grande Valley that covered nearly 9 million square feet. No evidence of agricultural intensification on a comparable scale exists anywhere in the Sierra Sin Agua.

Instead, small groups of Hisat'sinom there seem to have followed a strategy of cultivating fields scattered over large areas, investing the least amount of labor they could. Rock alignments in the Sierra Sin Agua might best be viewed as examples of agricultural "extensification"—that is, of farmers trying to spread the risk of dry-land agriculture over the largest area possible, rather than concentrating their effort in a single, well-designed, well-maintained field. This was probably a sensible strategy in a place where variation in local rainfall, rather than the fertility of the land, often dictated agricultural success.

My research on the CO Bar Ranch also turned up some hints about exactly how and when ancient farmers planted their crops. When I measured soil depth and soil moisture, some interesting patterns emerged.

The soils of the CO Bar Ranch are quite shallow. Over most of the study area, soil depths range from 6 to 20 inches and average only about 8.5 inches. Normally, this would be far too shallow for growing maize. But most soils in the CO Bar area benefit from what lies above and below them. At the base of the soil is an impervious

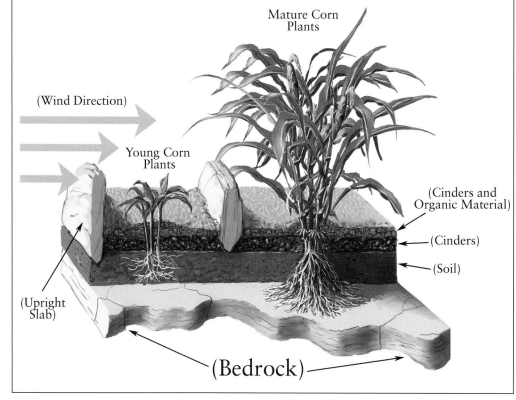

Figure 16.3. Ancient techniques of maize cultivation on the CO Bar Ranch. The corn plants are growing in a layer of soil sandwiched between cinders above and impervious bedrock below, protected from wind by upright stone slabs.

layer of Kaibab limestone, which keeps moisture from percolating too far down to be reached by the roots of crops. Above the soil lies a layer of Sunset Crater cinders, which prevent the rapid evaporation of soil moisture. Sandwiched between these two layers, local soils appear uniquely suited for retaining the sparse moisture that falls in both winter and summer.

I was able to confirm this supposition by testing soil moisture directly, using an electronic soil moisture meter. In the late spring, I found that soil wetted by winter snow and rain retained a considerable amount of moisture even weeks after the last precipitation. Indeed, where soil met bedrock, I obtained readings of complete saturation. I also saw that areas with the deepest soil gave drier readings and lacked rock alignments and other signs of farming. This counterintuitive result is probably best explained by the depth of the moisture-retaining bedrock in different places. When bedrock lies far below the surface, moisture seeps lower into the

soil and is unavailable to the relatively shallow roots of corn plants.

High soil moisture readings in late April suggested that ancient cultivators planted their corn shortly after the last frost of spring, which in this area usually strikes around the first week of May. At that time, enough soil moisture would have remained from winter storms to allow maize seeds to germinate and begin growing. With a few well-timed summer rains, maize could have grown to maturity and been harvested around the time of the first frost, which nowadays comes in October. This seasonal timing of planting and harvesting would have resembled that of the modern Hopis, who practice a similar strategy of dry-land farming in fields about 50 miles to the northeast.

By examining potsherds associated with the rock alignment fields on the CO Bar Ranch and with structures adjacent to them, I was able to date the fields to two broad time periods. The first was from around 1070 CE, roughly when the Sunset

Figure 16.4. Hopi farmer in a field of maize plants, 1875, probably near the pueblo of Sichomovi.

square feet. The later ones ran to about 51,000 square feet—more than 10 times larger. A major change had obviously taken place in the scale of cultivation.

Possible explanations for this change are many, and at present I have no definite answer. With population growing in the Wupatki area, increasing amounts of land probably had to be tilled. Individual families might have grown larger, too, producing more workers to clear and cultivate larger fields. It is also possible that the larger field sizes reflect the cumulative effects of farming over many decades. Although the thin soils on the CO Bar Ranch are good at retaining moisture, they are not particularly fertile, and repeated cultivation would have exhausted their nutrients fairly quickly. Declining soil fertility might have caused people to move their field locations often, especially in the later period of occupation, when they tried to cultivate increasingly marginal areas like the CO Bar Ranch. Rock alignments would have become spread over a large area as farmers tried to maintain agricultural productivity in the face of rapidly diminishing yields.

The story of ancient farmers on the CO Bar Ranch is one of ingenious and successful adaptation to an extremely challenging environment. Eight hundred years after Hisat'sinom cultivators planted their fields for the last time, we can still appreciate the struggle and determination represented by their humble lines of stone.

Gregory B. Brown is principal and senior archaeologist at Logan Simpson Design in Tempe, Arizona, an environmental consulting and landscape architecture firm.

Crater volcano erupted, until about 1140. The second spanned the years from 1140 to about 1220, when residence in the entire Wupatki area came to an end.

Comparing field sizes from the two periods, I was startled by their disparity. Among the fields that could be dated, the early ones averaged about 5,000

Figure 17.1. Hopi-Tewa potter, Nampeyo, around 1906. Hopi-Tewas descend from Tewa people who, around 1700, migrated from the northern Rio Grande region to join the First Mesa Hopi community, where they accepted the Hopi way of life.

Pottery of the Sierra Sin Agua

Kelley Hays-Gilpin and Christian E. Downum

At first, locally made pottery of the Sierra Sin Agua is difficult to see as one strolls through the ruins of a Hisat'sinom village. Small fragments of brown and red pots blend easily with the earth tones of clay soils. Next to showier black-on-white and red-on-orange pottery imported from neighboring regions, local jars and bowls at first glance seem plain and drab. But look more closely—this warm-hued pottery displays a pleasing range of mottled colors caused by the touch of fuel, air, and fire. Delicate pieces broken from finely polished bowls attest to the skill of potters who shaped subtle beauty and coaxed elegant function from materials readily at hand.

The earliest pottery in the Sierra Sin Agua, made around 600 CE, consisted of small, lightly polished brown vessels, embodying a simpler technology than those evolving elsewhere on the Colorado Plateau. Archaeologists classify this pottery as Alameda Brown Ware (plate 17), and it endured, with slow changes and refinements, for as long as the Hisat'sinom lived around the San Francisco Peaks. Its makers, people whom archaeologists traditionally referred to as the Sinagua, lived on the southeastern side of the peaks. Like other Native peoples throughout the Southwest, they shaped clay into myriad forms: bowls, jars, ladles, pitchers, cooking pots, effigy vessels, spindle whorls (small weights that helped weavers spin cotton thread on a wooden spindle), animal and human figurines, beads, pendants, and pipes.

The makers of Alameda Brown Ware formed their pots from locally available volcanic clays, to which they added temper, a nonplastic material such as sand that helped prevent the clay from cracking as it dried. Tempering materials consisted of whatever was available nearby, reflecting the diverse geology of the Flagstaff area. Common tempers included volcanic ash, tuff, sanidine crystals, quartz or basalt sand, crushed basalt, and crushed potsherds. Potters made Alameda Brown Ware vessels by the "paddle and anvil" technique, first building up coils of clay and then shaping and thinning them with a wooden paddle, which they struck against a stone or ceramic anvil held on the inside of the pot.

Alameda Brown Ware is unusual in that although potters sometimes polished the interiors of bowls

Figure 17.2. Ancient pottery-making tools from the Sierra Sin Agua. *Top*: anvils, the two on the left of limestone, the one on the right of basalt. *Center*: wooden paddle for smoothing clay coils against an anvil. *Bottom right*: polishing stones.

Figure 17.3. San Francisco Mountain Gray Ware jars and a mug (front left).

using smooth, water-rounded pebbles, they rarely painted or decoratively textured these vessels. Instead, they left them smooth and plain. Sometimes the makers smoothed a red slip—a slurry of clay—over a vessel's exterior as it dried, finishing it by rubbing it to a light polish with a smooth stone.

Makers of Alameda Brown Ware fired their pots in what is called an "oxidizing" atmosphere— that is, in such a way that air flowed freely through the mound of firewood forming the "kiln." The behavior of iron-rich volcanic clays under such firing conditions, which could not be tightly controlled, produced subtle variations in color, from brown and red to black. Darkened patches known as fire clouds formed where fuel wood touched a vessel wall or came close enough to produce an oxygen-poor or carbon-rich microenvironment at the vessel's surface.

Two of the most common types of Alameda Brown Ware are what archaeologists have labeled Sunset Brown and Sunset Red. People probably carried and stored water in red-slipped Sunset Red jars, and they likely served food in Sunset Red bowls. Both types contain shiny black particles of volcanic ash from the Sunset Crater eruption. Because volcanic ash is hard and angular, ash-tempered pottery is especially strong and resists cracking from stresses such as the thermal shock that comes when a vessel is used for cooking.

Archaeologists named ancient people living on the northwest side of the San Francisco Peaks a separate culture, the Cohonina, partly because they made and used pottery different from that of their Sinagua neighbors. Now called San Francisco Mountain Gray Ware, this pottery is gray, thin, and grittier than Alameda Brown Ware. Cohonina potters usually selected iron-poor clays and added sand as temper. They, too, used the paddle and anvil technique to thin their vessels, but then potters scraped them on both sides with a shaped potsherd or piece of gourd rind, leaving parallel striations. They fired the pots in pits covered with wood and charcoal to create an oxygen-poor atmosphere. This

Figure 17.4. Tusayan White Ware vessels. The piece at bottom center is a bird effigy jar.

"reducing" atmosphere generally turned the vessels gray, with splotches of black.

Cohonina potters made jars, pitchers, and bowls in simple but elegant shapes. Often they left the surfaces plain, but sometimes the maker applied a thin, red clay wash after the pot was fired. Because this slip is prone to dissolving or wearing away, researchers call the type Deadmans Fugitive Red (plate 16). Rarely, Cohonina potters painted bowl interiors with a plant-based paint. The designs resemble those from the Kayenta Pueblo area to the northeast, but Cohonina paint is often dark gray rather than true black, and the designs are simpler. Apparently, Cohonina people were satisfied with the subtle contrast between dark paint and gray background; they never tried to increase the contrast by adding a white slip on which to paint the darker designs.

Differences between San Francisco Mountain Gray Ware and Alameda Brown Ware are greater than the immediately obvious ones of color and surface treatment. For example, pitchers make up about 20 percent of all known San Francisco Mountain Gray Ware vessels but are almost nonexistent in Alameda Brown Ware. Alameda Brown Ware pots tend to be wider and shorter than those of San Francisco Mountain Gray Ware. The height-to-diameter ratios of the wares form two distinct statistical populations, with little overlap. We suspect that the development of pottery territories coincided with a sense of cultural identity, although local identities were probably more complex and dynamic than the simplifying terms Sinagua and Cohonina imply.

The Hisat'sinom of the Sierra Sin Agua, self-reliant, made most of their own pottery. Yet to

Figure 17.5. Mesoamerican design elements on pottery, textiles, and rock art from the Sierra Sin Agua and the Verde Valley, about 1140–1220 CE. *Left:* wall mosaics at the ancient site of Mitla in the Mexican state of Oaxaca. *Right, top to bottom:* Flagstaff Black-on-white bowl, about 1140–1220; painted cotton textile from Hidden House Ruin, about 1200; petroglyph near Citadel Pueblo, about 1200.

greater or lesser extents, they also acted as consumers of pottery, importing vessels from their neighbors in all directions. Especially popular were the beautiful, intricately painted, black-on-white and black-on-red bowls and jars manufactured to the north and east.

Potters of the Kayenta tradition, ancestors of the modern Hopi people, made their wares mostly in the vicinity of Black Mesa, a massive plateau looming over the modern town of Kayenta, Arizona, across the Little Colorado River northeast of the Sierra Sin Agua. Neighboring peoples valued

Figure 17.6. Tusayan Gray Ware vessels. The large jar at center and several of the small pots have "corrugated" surfaces.

Kayenta pottery highly, and ancestral Hopi potters over time exported hundreds of thousands of their pots to outlying regions. At Hisat'sinom ruins in the Sierra Sin Agua, 5 to 25 percent of all pottery consists of Kayenta wares.

Imported pottery of the Kayenta tradition came in white, gray, and red or orange. Tusayan White Ware, consisting mostly of food serving bowls and water storage jars, was polished and then decorated with plant-based paint. When Kayenta potters fired their carbon-rich, iron-poor clay in a reducing atmosphere, they got white backgrounds that contrasted sharply with the overlying black paint. Their intricate designs generally took geometric shapes, with individual elements repeated and rotated in wide bands running across the outsides of jars and the insides of bowls. Many of the design elements, which crosscut media such as ceramics, rock art, and textiles, can be traced ultimately to decorative traditions of Mesoamerica (see chapter 18).

The gray Kayenta pottery that shows up in

Sierra Sin Agua archaeological sites, Tusayan Gray Ware, was fashioned from the same clay and with the same techniques as Tusayan White Ware, but these cooking and storage jars had coarser sand temper and rougher surface textures. To decorate the surfaces, potters often pinched or indented the coils in a manner called "corrugation." The coarse temper and corrugations might have enhanced the cooking performance of these pots.

Two kinds of decorated red and orange pottery were also popular imports to the Sierra Sin Agua (plate 18). People carried San Juan Red Ware, produced in southeastern Utah, far and wide perhaps as early as the 700s CE. Its most common type, Deadmans Black-on-red, is fine, thin walled, and hard, with a well-polished red slip and bold black designs. The painted designs usually include long parallel lines to which are attached interlocking solid shapes such as hooked triangles.

Sometime in the 1000s, San Juan Red Ware was replaced by Tsegi Orange Ware, whose makers used

Figure 17.7. Little Colorado White Ware vessels.

an iron-rich clay that turned bright orange when fired. By the 1100s these potters had developed a three-color ("polychrome") style of decoration, featuring designs in red and black painted over the orange background (plate 22). To modern eyes, it is easy to understand the appeal these colorful red and orange pots must have held for Hisat'sinom who bartered for them.

One last source of imported pottery was the Hopi Buttes area along the Little Colorado River, south of the Hopi Mesas. Potters there made black-on-white serving vessels and gray, corrugated utility jars. Archaeologist Amy Douglass used sophisticated chemical and geological techniques to match Little Colorado White Ware pottery to a clay that outcrops in the eroded badlands near modern Dilkon, Arizona. This iron-rich clay fires dark gray in a

reducing atmosphere, and nothing a potter can do—no amount of polishing, no special firing techniques—will make it appear white. To make a white pot from this clay, the maker must cover it with a white slip before it is painted and fired. All Little Colorado White Wares exhibit a white, chalky clay slip, probably made from nearby sources of kaolin, a pure white clay.

One might expect that all these beautifully painted white, red, and orange imports—displaying some of the most complicated and skillful painting in all of ancient North America—would have inspired Sinagua and Cohonina potters to decorate their own brown ware pots. In fact, they seldom did so. They knew how to paint pottery and had access to the necessary pigments, but at most they emulated the simplest designs of their Kayenta neighbors and

Endangered Pottery

Ancient pottery tells us a great deal about the daily lives and interactions of the people who made and used it. To the Hopi people, potsherds are footprints of their ancestors. At each place where the clans stopped during their migrations, they broke their old pots and made new ones, so that those who came later could read the story of their journey.

Sadly, thousands of pots and potsherds are removed from the land and sold for profit every year. Virtually all their potential information is destroyed when they are wrenched from their original locations, or proveniences. A pot in an art gallery or on a collector's mantle is all but useless if its provenience is unknown. Potsherds made into earrings or refrigerator magnets and sold in flea markets and online auction sites no longer have the ability to communicate about the people who made and used them.

As you visit archaeological sites and walk the ancient landscapes of the Hisat'sinom, please leave potsherds and other artifacts where you find them. Enjoy their beauty by picking them up and looking at them, but always place the artifacts back on the spot where they were resting. Don't place artifacts in a pile to help other visitors see them; this, too, disturbs the provenience, and it may lead others to help themselves to a souvenir. Taking or disturbing arti-facts also violates federal, state, and tribal laws, and perpetrators are subject to fines and other penalties, including imprisonment. It is important not to purchase ancient pottery, even if it comes from private land. Doing so encourages additional looting.

Footprints of the ancestors were meant to teach us across the generations. If we recognize and respect that simple principle, they can continue to do so for a long time to come.

---

never developed a locally distinct style. Sinagua pot-ters occasionally painted a few white, broad-line geometric designs on vessel exteriors, imitating Hohokam pots for a brief time in the late 1000s and early 1100s. Cohonina artisans now and then painted relatively simple designs covering only a small fraction of the vessel.

Why did the Sinagua and Cohonina people never embrace their neighbors' pottery painting tra-ditions? Perhaps they simply invested greater effort in other media, such as textiles, tattoos, or jewelry, that for them more effectively communicated infor-mation about social identity. Perhaps they simply valued the distinctiveness and subtle attractions of the marks made by fire on their own local pottery. Many Hopi potters today say the fire clouds and "blush" colors of plain pottery are even more beau-tiful than painted designs, because the marks left by the fire show that the pot is alive. Maybe the trans-actions that brought the decorated pots to Sierra Sin Agua villages helped maintain social and economic ties with distant neighbors. Pottery is just one of many items for which people of the region traded

(see chapter 19), and it is difficult to know whether the pottery itself or something contained in the vessels was the primary impetus for trade.

Neither Alameda Brown Ware nor San Francisco Mountain Gray Ware survived into his-toric times. But what happened to the people who made them? When archaeologists use ceramics as the basis for defining social groups, they can lose track of the makers when the ceramics no longer appear at archaeological sites. If some thirteenth-century Sinagua people moved to the Hopi Mesas, for example, did the potters among them abandon their distinctive pottery-making techniques and adopt Kayenta methods that were perhaps better suited to local sedimentary clays? Is the contem-porary Hopi aesthetic appreciation of fire clouds and orange mottling on their pottery a distant echo of Sinagua tastes for fire-clouded pottery, perhaps the legacy of long-ago immigrants to the Hopi Mesas? These questions deserve future attention, and collaborative research among scientists and Hopi artists might be a productive way to begin.

Figure 18.1. Hopi man seated at a small, upright loom, about 1898.

From Seed Pod to Shirt

Cotton Textiles in the Sierra Sin Agua

Lisa Folb

Fine cotton cloth, expertly woven and luxuriously soft, surely made a rare and valuable commodity for ancient people in the northern reaches of the Southwest, where cotton is hard to grow. Pueblo Indians in historic times associated this white, fluffy stuff symbolically with clouds and breath, and by extension with sacred concepts of rain and spirit. In the Sierra Sin Agua, Hisat'sinom weavers took cotton bolls—mere seed pods—and turned them into complex and beautiful pieces of cloth.

Cotton was one of several tropical plants that Native peoples of the Southwest imported from Mesoamerica and adapted for desert cultivation. Residents of the southern deserts of the Southwest grew cotton earliest, beginning around 500 CE, thanks to a long growing season and water from irrigation. The plant came much later to the northern Southwest, where only a few places offered the right combination of warm temperatures and adequate moisture. Cotton cultivation may have begun there around 700 CE, but it did not become widespread until after 1100—in the Sierra Sin Agua, after the eruption of the Sunset Crater volcano.

We know these Hisat'sinom raised cotton and wove cloth because they left behind many traces of the plants, weaving tools, and the cloth itself at their pit house and pueblo ruins. In dry environments like those of the deep, rubble-filled rooms at Wupatki Pueblo and the alcoves of Walnut Canyon, archaeologists have uncovered well-preserved cotton fibers, seeds, bolls, and stems, along with ancient cotton thread and fragments of cloth. Microscopic analyses of soil samples from Hisat'sinom farm plots occasionally reveal cotton pollen. Burned vegetal remains from ancient structures sometimes include bits of cotton plants, especially seeds.

To create a piece of cotton cloth, the weaver first had to spin raw cotton into thread by hand. At Wupatki Pueblo, archaeologists found long, straight sticks that served as spindles, and from Wupatki and many other sites come a variety of small, perforated weights known as spindle whorls. These added weight to the spindle, making it easier to draw fibers out of the mass of raw cotton and twist them into thread by turning the spindle. Spindle whorls in the Sierra Sin Agua were mostly flat disks made from potsherds or wood, with a hole drilled in the middle, and small, compact, beadlike forms modeled from clay and fired. The modeled spindle whorls resemble ones found throughout the Hohokam area of southern Arizona and south into Mesoamerica. The profusion of spindle whorls in Sierra Sin Agua sites shows that the spinning of cotton thread, and presumably weaving as well, was widespread.

Hisat'sinom of the Sierra Sin Agua wove cotton cloth on vertical looms suspended from roof beams and anchored to small holes in the floors of kivas and other rooms. Carefully aligned holes for this purpose have been uncovered at pueblos such as Juniper Terrace and Nalakihu. Weavers also likely used other kinds of looms, such as the small backstrap loom, one end of which was tied to a wall or

Figure 18.2. Weaving tools and cotton from Wupatki Pueblo. The circular objects are wood and clay spindle whorls. Other wooden objects are a piece of a loom bar (far left), a shed rod (top), and a spindle (center). Bottom: a fragment of woven cotton cloth and raw cotton.

post while the other was secured to the weaver's body by means of a strap worn across the back.

The basic purpose of a loom is to keep a vertical set of threads, the warp, under tension so that another set of threads, the weft, can be passed horizontally over and under the warp to create a pattern. On the upright loom, a beam called a shed rod separates the warp threads to distinguish those that the weft will pass over from those it will pass under. As the weaver inserts weft threads through the warp threads, he or she uses a batten—a thin, flat piece of wood—to widen the gap in the warp. By tying a rod now known as a heddle to warp threads according to a pattern, the weaver can more readily separate the warp with the batten and thus repeat design elements more easily. Excavations at Wupatki Pueblo turned up remains of battens, heddles, and

shed rods, further evidence that people there wove on upright looms.

Wupatki is also the source of by far the largest collection of ancient cotton cloth from anywhere in the Sierra Sin Agua, a sample that encompasses a diversity of Southwestern weaving styles. I examined 50 well-preserved specimens of cloth from Wupatki and found that 42 of them consisted of what is called balanced plain weave. In this simplest of patterns, the weaver passes a single weft thread over and under each individual warp thread, pushing each new weft thread down against the previous one. As at Wupatki, the majority of ancient cotton fabrics throughout the Southwest are balanced plain weave.

The other cloth fragments from Wupatki displayed more complex and sophisticated patterns

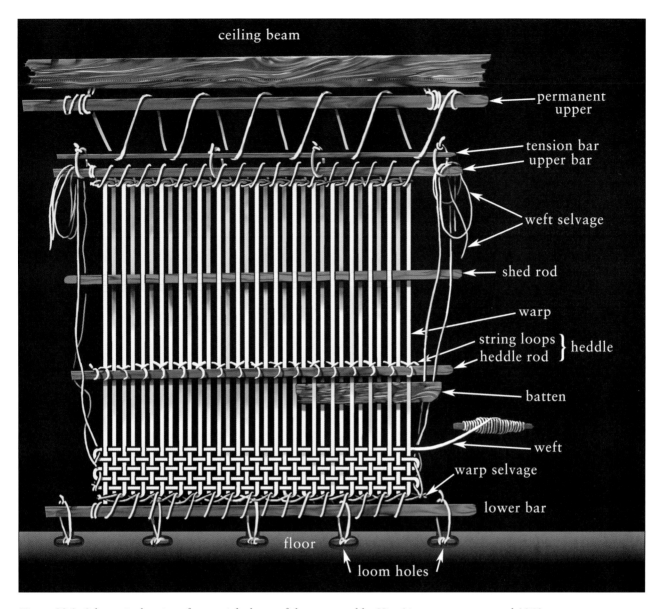

Figure 18.3. Schematic drawing of an upright loom of the type used by Hisat'sinom weavers around 1150 CE.

created by varying the way the weft passed under and over the warp. Four of the specimens were twill weaves, a pattern in which the weft extends over two or more warp threads (or vice versa) at a time, creating diagonal ribs or lines. The fabric used to make modern denim jeans, for example, is a twill weave.

Of the last four specimens, one was a warp-faced plain weave, meaning that warp threads outnumbered the weft threads to the point of obscuring them on the finished surface of the textile. Another exemplified a pattern called tapestry, a weft-faced (wefts outnumbering warps) plain weave in which the

weaver uses color blocks to create a pattern. A third piece of cloth combined the twill and tapestry techniques, and the fourth consisted of weft-wrap openwork. This is essentially a plain weave pattern, but the weaver winds thread around several warp and previously inserted weft threads to pull them apart and create decorative holes in the fabric.

My analysis of the cloth from Wupatki Pueblo formed part of a larger study in which I looked at the way weave types varied geographically throughout the Southwest from about 1100 to 1300 CE. I wanted to learn which regional traditions Wupatki's

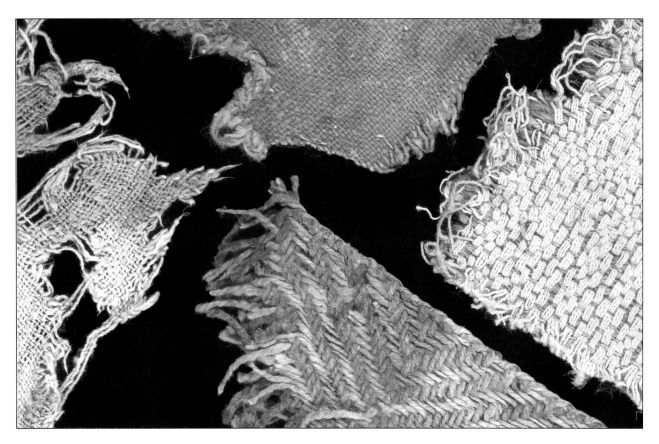

Figure 18.4. Examples of ancient woven cloth from Wupatki Pueblo. The piece at bottom is a herringbone twill; the other three are plain weave.

weavers might have drawn on when they made their fabrics. I examined the characteristics of 945 pieces of ancient cloth from five major regions, the valleys of the San Juan, Little Colorado, Verde, Salt-Gila, and Mimbres Rivers. Two correlations stood out. Archaeological sites in the San Juan and Little Colorado valleys—both to the northeast of the Sierra Sin Agua—produced the greatest number of fabric remains showing twill patterns. The Verde River valley, just southwest of the San Francisco Peaks, and the Salt-Gila and Mimbres areas, far to the south and southeast, respectively, produced the largest number of warp-faced plain weaves and specimens incorporating weft-wrap openwork.

If these differences reflect distinct cultural traditions at work, perhaps on either side of a rough north-south divide, then the twill cloth found at Wupatki, together with its examples of warp-faced plain weave and weft-wrap openwork, suggest that its weavers were familiar with fabrics from both

directions. With their diversity of weaving styles, perhaps the textile makers of Wupatki arrived there from many different places, or perhaps they had access to finished cotton cloth through extensive trade networks. Given abundant archaeological evidence that Wupatki's residents grew, spun, and wove their own fabrics, I am inclined to the first scenario, although long-distance trade for cotton cloth is certainly possible.

I also examined what I considered to be "exceptional" fabrics, which had to meet either of two criteria. Among the twilled fabrics, I looked for pieces showing a particular kind of complex pattern that could have been created only with the use of four or more heddles. Alternatively, an exceptional piece had to show a thread count—the number of warp and weft threads in an inch of cloth—of greater than 40 threads per inch. To achieve such a high count, a weaver must spin a fine thread, rig the loom so that the warp threads are closely spaced,

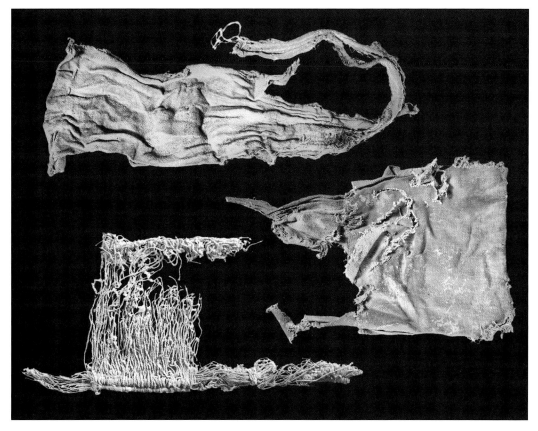

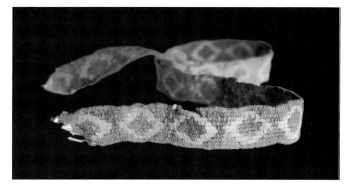

Figure 18.5. Finished cloth items from Wupatki and Honanki Pueblos. *Top, clockwise:* breechcloth, unidentified piece, string skirt. *Left:* bag. *Right:* belt.

and then weave the wefts equally close together. Creating such a densely woven cloth is time consuming, and weavers would have invested such time and effort only to create high-value pieces, perhaps for trade or ceremonial use.

After averaging warp and weft thread counts for each of the 945 pieces in my sample, I found just six that had exceptionally high counts, and two of these were from Wupatki. Indeed, at 53 warp and weft threads per inch, they ranked at the very top of the sample. Only three specimens met my second criterion, a twill pattern woven with at least four heddles, and one of the three came from Wupatki Pueblo.

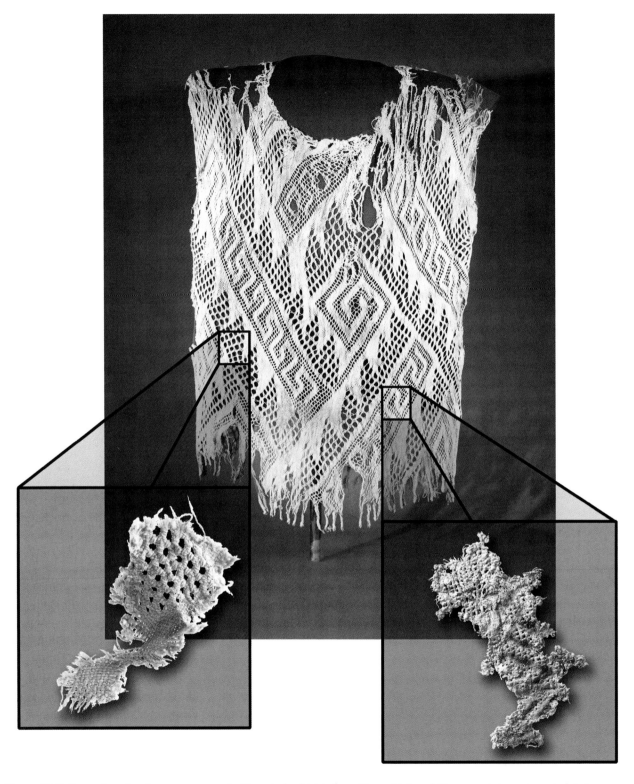

Figure 18.6. Examples of weft-wrap openwork. The whole shirt is from Tonto National Monument, in east-central Arizona. The archaeological specimens, corresponding to portions of the shirt, are from Honanki Pueblo in the Verde Valley. Similar pieces have been recovered from Wupatki.

The presence of both high-density and complex twilled fabrics was unique to Wupatki; no other site in the sample had both. These pieces are among the Southwest's most finely woven examples of cotton cloth, and their presence at Wupatki is consistent with other lines of evidence showing that this was a place that both attracted and produced valuable items (see also chapters 11 and 19).

Ancient Southwestern cotton fabrics are remarkable creations that reflect the considerable skill, ingenuity, and dedication of their makers. Cotton was not an easy crop to grow in the Flagstaff area, where much of the terrain lies at relatively high, cool elevations and rainfall is scarce. Still, in the decades after the eruption of the Sunset Crater volcano, cotton cloth became an important part of local life. Residents of some places in the Sierra Sin Agua, especially Wupatki Pueblo, participated fully in a complex web of actions, styles, and meanings that surrounded the weaving and use of cotton cloth.

Lisa Folb is a project manager for a consulting firm in Washington, D.C., whose archaeological studies have taken her from the lush woodlands of the northeastern United States to the deserts of the Southwest. A native of South Africa, she grew up with a British grandmother who taught her the skills of fabric and needlework—skills that intersected with her interest in archaeology to lead her to the study of preserved Southwestern textiles.

Figure 19.1. Exotic items from the Sierra Sin Agua, around 1050 to 1300 CE, including ornaments of shell, turquoise, and argillite.

Exotic Goods in the Sierra Sin Agua

Saul L. Hedquist

Broken remnants of pots, worn-out grinding tools, and chips of stone litter the ground at archaeological sites, telling a story of common items crafted from local materials that never traveled very far. Rarer artifacts, rich with symbolism and carried from great distances away, tell a different story— one of far-reaching relationships between the ancient peoples of the Sierra Sin Agua and their neighbors. Indeed, the region formed a crossroads for the transport of valuable commodities, from shell jewelry to mineral pigments, from copper bells to living macaws. All changed hands in a lively system of trade and gift-giving that existed throughout the U.S. Southwest and northern Mexico.

In ancient times, the acquisition of exotic items required great effort, risk, training, or expense. People needed special knowledge about where to obtain such objects or the raw materials to make them, how to manufacture and care for them, and how they should properly be used. As a result, these artifacts constituted the most powerful, sacred, and valuable items in the Hisat'sinom world. Many ended up buried beneath the floors of pueblo rooms, cached in special places like niches in kivas, or buried in their owners' graves.

Among the more common and yet most exotic artifacts of the ancient Sierra Sin Agua were ornaments made of shell. People wore shell as early as Archaic times, more than 2,000 years ago, but its use increased greatly following the eruption of the Sunset Crater volcano in the late eleventh century. Most of the shell originated along the Gulf of California near Kino Bay in Sonora, Mexico, or along the Pacific Ocean in southern California— both a long way from today's northern Arizona. Travelers carrying shell from the Gulf of California likely followed ancient trade routes passing through the Hohokam area in southern Arizona. Items from the California coast, mostly large specimens of abalone (*Haliotis*; plate 25), arrived by an overland route roughly coincident with modern Interstate Highway 40.

Native peoples of the Southwest prized marine shell in part because it symbolized the power and mystery of the ocean. The ocean figures prominently in creation stories of the Hopis, who regard water as a sacred substance and the spiritual essence of a person and of the Katsinam, the spirit messengers. The Zunis believe that Zuni Pueblo, the "middle place," is equally distant from the four great oceans of the world. In southern Arizona, Tohono O'odham boys making the transition to adulthood undertook long-distance pilgrimages to the Gulf of California. Ancient Mimbres people of southwestern New Mexico, living nearly 300 miles from any ocean, decorated their pottery with vivid pictures of ocean life, including scenes of men swimming with fishes and spearing what might be a whale. Surely the ocean and things that symbolized it, such as seashells, were profoundly important to the Hisat'sinom.

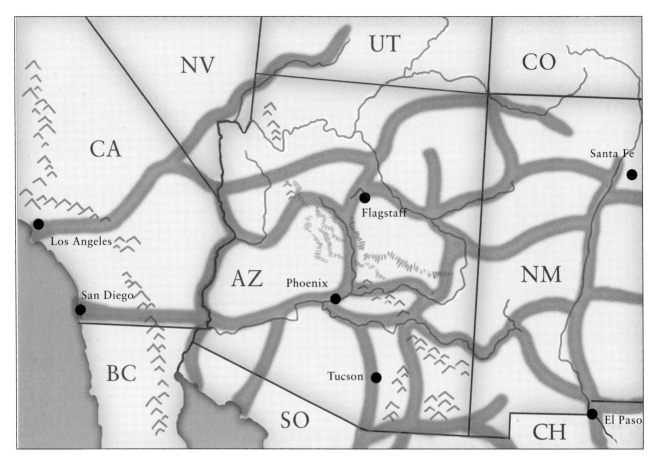

Figure 19.2. Ancient trade routes through the U.S. Southwest and northern Mexico.

Generally, people fashioned shells of relatively large species into bracelets and large pendants. They converted small shells into beads, rings, and smaller pendants (plate 26). The most common kind of shell bracelet came from bivalves of the genus *Glycymeris*. Small olive (*Olivella*) shells contributed most of the beads. Apparently, ancient people also collected fossilized specimens of an extinct form of sand dollar (*Encope grandis*), although we do not know exactly how they used them. Archaeologists have uncovered both worked and unworked shell at sites in the Sierra Sin Agua, suggesting that local people made some of their own jewelry and imported the rest.

We do not know all the situations in which people wore their shell jewelry, but at the least they probably displayed it during special events such as religious rituals and public ceremonies. Shell adornments might have signaled a person's social status, ethnicity, or membership in a religious or social organization. Archaeologist James Bayman has proposed that shell bracelets in the low deserts of the Southwest symbolized the ethnic status of being Hohokam. Perhaps this was true in the Sierra Sin Agua as well; shell bracelets were most common there during the years marked by the use of Hohokam-style ball courts and are concentrated at sites located near these features.

To measure the relationship between architecture and ornament, researcher Tracy Murphy calculated ratios of shell artifacts to plain-ware potsherds for a large sample of archaeological sites in the Sierra Sin Agua. She found shell to be 17 times more abundant at sites within three-quarters of a mile of a ball court than at sites farther away. The largest proportions of shell—97 to 484 shell items per 10,000 plain-ware potsherds—came from villages within sight of the ball courts at Ridge Ruin, Winona Village, and Juniper Terrace. The average shell quantity for sites near ball courts was 102 per

Figure 19.3. Modern examples of the shell species used by the Hisat'sinom in the Sierra Sin Agua. In the top row, the two center specimens are the conch *Strombus galeatus*, and the two at right are *Murex nigritus*, both of which were used as trumpets.

10,000 potsherds; the average for non–ball court sites was 6.

The sheer numbers of shell items found at the region's larger sites are impressive, sometimes exceeding even those at purely Hohokam sites to the south. At Wupatki Pueblo, excavators unearthed more than 1,600 pieces of shell jewelry made from more than 30 species. Two of the most spectacular finds were large shell trumpets, one fashioned from a large, pinkish brown conch (*Strombus galeatus*) and the other from the black-striped, spiny univalve *Murex nigritus*. People undoubtedly heard these trumpets during Wupatki's most sacred ceremonies. For the Hopis and Zunis, the long, low notes of shell trumpets announced certain religious gatherings and gave voice to the plumed serpent that figured in important ceremonies. *Strombus* trumpets served a similar function in indigenous societies from Mexico to Peru.

Not only shell but also stone played a decora-tive role in the Sierra Sin Agua. The most abundant stone ornaments are those made of argillite, a stone metamorphosed from clay and colored reddish by iron. Argillite's beautiful, warm tones range from deep maroon to almost orange, and it sometimes includes flecks and bands of white that give it a mottled or striped effect. A primary source of argillite is the Del Rio mine, situated in the Chino Valley of north-central Arizona.

From argillite, ancient people made rings, beads, pendants, and a variety of plugs that they wore through perforations in their noses, cheeks, or lips (plates 28, 29). They also carved it into human and animal effigies, including imitation seashells and shell bracelets. Small, precisely cut and beveled pieces of argillite adorned shell-backed mosaics. At some sites in the Sierra Sin Agua, archaeologists have uncovered many unworked specimens of argillite, suggesting that local people imported raw stone along with finished ornaments.

Figure 19.4. Hopi girls at Shungopavi, four of them wearing shell bead and pendant necklaces, around 1901.

Like shell artifacts, argillite appears unevenly across the region. Hisat'sinom living east of the San Francisco Peaks especially treasured this stone. We do not know why, but we can speculate about its symbolic meanings. The deep red of argillite resembles blood, and the wearing of decorative plugs made from it required that a part of the human body be cut, removed, or enlarged to accommodate them. Unlike other jewelry, these plugs became part of the wearer's body; perhaps this incorporation added to argillite's mystique and helped define its association with certain cultural groups. According to Leigh Kuwanwisiwma, Hopi men of the Eagle clan used to wear ornaments in their noses, in my view possibly a continuation of ancient practices in the Sierra Sin Agua.

Another important stone was turquoise, but unlike argillite, it was never very abundant at Hisat'sinom villages. Likely sources include ancient mines near Santa Fe, New Mexico, and Kingman, Arizona, although it is possible that some turquoise came from southern Arizona and perhaps as far away as Nevada and Colorado. Artisans made beads, pendants (plate 27), embellishments for argillite plugs (plate 28), and animal and human effigies out of the stone, goods that the Hisat'sinom seem to have imported rather than made locally. Researchers have found few unworked specimens of turquoise in the Sierra Sin Agua.

Turquoise might have been important to the Hisat'sinom for two primary reasons: it evoked the color of both sky and water, and Mesoamerican peoples prized it and went to great lengths to import it from mines throughout the U.S. Southwest. Whatever their reasons, ancient people of the Sierra Sin Agua clearly valued the stone

Figure 19.5. Jet buttons from Wupatki National Monument, probably used around 1100 to 1140 CE, resting atop pieces of raw jet.

highly. Most of the pieces we find are very small, and some show signs of having been conserved when people reworked broken pieces into new ornaments.

Other varieties of stone that people crafted into ornaments included jet, hematite, shale, travertine, limestone, steatite, and malachite. Fossils such as segments of crinoid stems sometimes served as beads. The jet ornaments are particularly fascinating. Jet is a form of lignite, a mineraloid (not a true mineral) formed by the hardening of carbon in ancient wood under extreme compression. Sources can be found in Utah, northern Arizona, and New Mexico. In the ancient Southwest, jet ornaments often take the distinctive form of rectangular or disk-shaped "buttons," each with one highly polished side (presumably the front) and a peculiar back showing small ridges and holes. We do not know how these items functioned, but they are extremely rare and perhaps held great importance. In addition to buttons, artists carved jet into animal

forms such as frogs. Jet artifacts occasionally served as the backing for mosaics of turquoise and other minerals, and jet itself was cut and ground into small, thin pieces for mosaics.

Again in the realm of stone, people across the Sierra Sin Agua imported a variety of powdered mineral pigments (plate 24), mainly azurite (deep blue), malachite (vibrant green), kaolin (pure white), and hematite (available in hues ranging from yellowish red to purple and sometimes found in a sparkling form). Pigments came from both surface and underground sources, many of which have likely been destroyed by modern mining. Some pigment minerals, such as hematite, are commonly found in sedimentary rock throughout the Sierra Sin Agua. Others are found only in southern Arizona and northern Mexico and could not have been synthesized or imitated with local materials.

People used pigments to paint their bodies and faces for rituals, to color their clothing, and to decorate objects like shell jewelry and ritual paraphernalia such as masks, altars, animal replicas, and wands. The rich colors of natural pigments were highly meaningful, symbolizing things such as water, the sky, the sun, purity, snow, blood, fire, and the cardinal directions. Pigments formed an indispensable element of social and religious action.

The Hisat'sinom imported living creatures as well—spectacular macaws native to Mesoamerican jungles. Traders carried these birds north through the Mimbres country in baskets rigged to be worn like backpacks. At the trading center of Paquimé, in the modern Mexican state of Chihuahua, ancient people bred macaws, but no firm evidence exists that residents of the U.S. Southwest ever raised the birds.

Researchers find two species of macaws at Sierra Sin Agua sites: the scarlet macaw (*Ara macao*), which inhabits jungles along the eastern coast of Mexico, some 1,200 miles distant, and the military macaw (*Ara militaris*), found in parts of northern Mexico. The scarlet macaw is a very large bird, some three feet long, half of which is tail feathers. It is strikingly beautiful, with iridescent feathers of red, blue, and yellow that, when turned in the light, show all the colors of the rainbow (plate 24, center). Military macaws are less brilliantly colored but have beautiful plumage nonetheless, mostly green on the body with blue feathers on the wings, a tuft of brilliant red at the beak, and long tail feathers of red tipped with green.

Remains of these gorgeous birds appear primarily at the larger sites in the Sierra Sin Agua, such as Wupatki Pueblo, Ridge Ruin, Winona Village, and Elden Pueblo. Wupatki alone yielded 685 macaw bones representing approximately 41 individual birds—more than one-fourth of all the macaws ever found at archaeological sites in the American Southwest. Judging from the number of macaws per room, Wupatki housed more than 10 times as many macaws as any site of the Chaco culture, including Pueblo Bonito.

Why did the Hisat'sinom seek out these exotic birds? The colors of their feathers symbolize the cardinal directions to Pueblo people today, and we are fairly certain that the feathers formed important parts of ceremonial costumes in the distant past. A rock shelter in Utah, for example, yielded a blanket made of scarlet macaw feathers. Hopi oral tradition

assigns to macaws an important role in the history of Wupatki Pueblo. In one story, a member of the Parrot clan is said to have been buried there with his parrots, a story perhaps corroborated by the archaeological discovery of a large number of macaw burials at Wupatki. At least 11 of the macaws there earned respectful burials of a type normally reserved for adult humans. One macaw, with a prayer feather attached to its foot, had been wrapped in cotton cloth and buried with a child. Three others had been placed in burial shrouds of yucca matting. People must have prized these affectionate, intelligent birds as more than just a source of colorful feathers.

Of all the exotic objects traded into the Sierra Sin Agua, copper bells, which were likely produced at a small number of smelting sites in western Mexico, were the most technologically sophisticated. Their makers employed a form of the lost wax technique in which the bells were cast in clay molds heated by wood or charcoal fires to about 2,000 degrees Fahrenheit. Modern engineers who have studied ancient copper bells marvel at the ingenuity of the early Mexican metallurgists, and the Hisat'sinom surely admired their skill as well.

Archaeologists have found copper bells at only 93 sites in the entire Southwest, for a total of around 630 specimens. Thirty of these come from the Sierra Sin Agua. Most of them are spherical, an inch or less in diameter, with a small copper loop at the top (plate 30). Archaeologists uncovered six such bells at Wupatki Pueblo and other examples at seven other sites. Nineteenth-century looters at Wupatki found a single example of a second type of bell, featuring raised ridges forming a face with a fanged mouth, perhaps depicting the Mesoamerican rain deity known as Tlaloc. A third type, with geometric decorations on the top half, came from Winona Village.

How were exotic goods other than shell distributed among sites in the Sierra Sin Agua? To find out, I applied Tracy Murphy's analytical methods to exotic artifacts of all types. I learned that exotic commodities existed in greater quantities at sites with large structures—kivas, plazas, and ball courts—used for religious ceremonies and other public gatherings. Archaeologists have discovered macaws only at large sites with places for public gatherings, and with two known exceptions, copper bells are also concentrated at such places. Turquoise unquestionably has its greatest concentration at substantial sites like Ridge Ruin, Wupatki, and Two Kivas Pueblo, as do mineral pigments.

But how can we know what this unequal distribution of exotic goods means? Traditionally, researchers lumped all kinds of exotics together as "prestige" goods and assumed that social and political elites exchanged them to forge alliances and seal agreements. Recently, a more nuanced view has emerged. Archaeologists now recognize that different kinds of exotic objects had different meanings and roles in ancient societies. Some exotic goods likely were considered "inalienable" possessions—that is, their significance adhered permanently to the person or group that acquired them. Other goods might have marked certain offices or positions, remaining with the office as its holders succeeded one another. Exotic goods were not simply wealth, and they did not necessarily pass only from one elite stratum to another.

The ancient peoples of the Sierra Sin Agua did not live by utilitarian goods alone, nor did they inhabit a world reaching only to the near horizon. They were connected to distant corners of the U.S. Southwest and Mexico, and their complex religious, social, and political lives required exotic items for many reasons. We are just beginning to understand the many possible ways in which people used and valued shell, argillite, turquoise, and many other items that were rare, beautiful, and difficult to obtain.

Saul L. Hedquist is a Ph.D. student at the University of Arizona. His research to date has focused on prehistoric social organization and exchange in the U.S. Southwest, particularly in northern Arizona.

Figure 20.1. O'Neill Crater, the site of New Caves Pueblo.

The Troubled End of Pueblo Life in the Sierra Sin Agua

Evidence from the Site of New Caves

John C. Whittaker and Kathryn Kamp

In the mid-1200s CE, something dramatic happened among the cinder cones of the Sierra Sin Agua: most people left their small farming hamlets and gathered in a few large villages. Within another 50 years, farming and pueblo life in the region vanished altogether. A landscape once home to thousands now lay empty, to be visited over the next six centuries only by hunters, travelers, nomadic bands, and descendants of former residents who came to remember the Hisat'sinom with shrines and religious offerings. Not until the late 1800s would large numbers of people live there again, this time Euro-American settlers who marveled at the remains of so many ancient pit house and pueblo communities.

Cycles of village reorganization, migration, and relocation were relatively common in the ancient Southwest, but even by that standard, the departure of the Hisat'sinom from the Sierra Sin Agua stands out as abrupt and puzzling. In less than two generations, a landscape where people had successfully lived and farmed for more than 500 years became vacant. What happened to uproot so many Hisat'sinom so quickly?

For several years we have been seeking answers to this question, concentrating our efforts in and around New Caves, an ancient pueblo and pit house settlement about 12 miles northeast of modern Flagstaff, Arizona. We are a long way from understanding all the factors leading to the Hisat'sinom migrations of the late 1200s, but we believe New

Caves offers important evidence that conflict or the threat of conflict was at least part of the story.

New Caves rests on the summit and southern slopes of O'Neill Crater, the rugged cinder cone of an extinct volcano rising about 300 feet above the surrounding terrain—one of hundreds of such cones in the sprawling San Francisco volcanic field. Just south of New Caves, the Rio de Flag cuts through a valley where Hisat'sinom lived in earlier years, finding readily available farmland and drinking water.

The pottery we find at New Caves tells us that people lived there only between about 1250 and 1300 CE. The site consists of small groups of structures totaling about 47 pueblo rooms, 25 pit houses, and 43 cave rooms hollowed out of the underlying volcanic cinders. Scattered among these are terraces, walls, and clearings for ephemeral rooms. A walled plaza and a large, square "community room," probably used for ceremonial gatherings, sit where the trail from below reaches the saddle of the peak. Halfway up the same trail lies Bench Pueblo, with another 20 pueblo rooms and pit structures. A few more small clusters of houses on the flanks of O'Neill Crater were also probably part of the community.

New Caves is one of only four substantial pueblo communities in the Sierra Sin Agua known to have been inhabited later than 1250. Two others, Elden and Turkey Hill Pueblos, are large, open-air

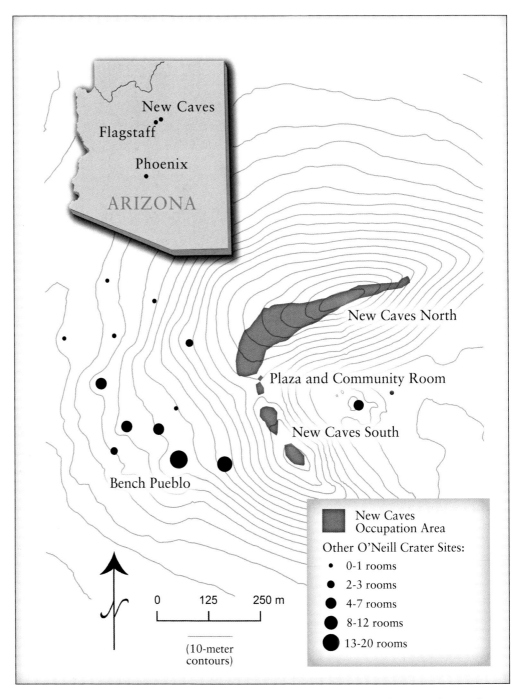

Figure 20.2. New Caves Crater, showing New Caves and Bench Pueblos and surrounding settlements on the slopes and summit of the crater.

settlements of several dozen rooms and pit structures each, both in the pine forest east of Elden Mountain, a volcanic dome near the San Francisco Peaks. The fourth is Old Caves, a community of around 90 pueblo rooms at the summit of a volcano some four miles west of New Caves.

The sites of New Caves and Old Caves got their

names because the nineteenth-century archaeologist Jesse Walter Fewkes, who first explored them, was fascinated by their cave rooms. Each site has a distinctive style of underground construction. At New Caves, people created cave rooms mostly by digging horizontally into the volcanic cliffs and then closing the excavated chambers with walls across the front.

Figure 20.3. Cave rooms at New Caves Pueblo.

New Caves are about the same size and have the same layouts as earlier hamlets on the valley floor. Apparently, when area residents moved there, they tried to retain continuity with their old way of life by echoing the plans of their previous homes. Similarly, a community room and a walled plaza provided spaces for community events, as they had in some earlier villages. Now, though, the house clusters were bunched more tightly in a much smaller area. People probably remained in their traditional family groups, but now they lived much closer together.

The view from the summit of O'Neill Crater is magnificent in all directions, but people's new homes atop an extinct volcano, besides being crowded, suffered other disadvantages. In summer the sun beat down on slopes stripped of trees for fuel and building. The wind howled across the rocks in gusts of 30 miles per hour or more, hurling blinding blasts of dust. During thunderstorms the crest of the cinder cone is vulnerable to lightning, making it a frightening place in which to loiter outdoors. In winter the barren slopes are cold and still windy.

Building their houses at New Caves, people tried to compensate for the tough conditions. Cave rooms in the cliff face offered good shelter for their day. Facing south, they caught the winter sun but tended to be shaded during the hottest parts of summer days. Many of the houses on the volcano's slopes were pit structures with their roofs at surface level, insulated by the earth against extreme heat and cold. Surrounding walls provided a windbreak and some shade around small, enclosed living areas. Such walled areas, unknown in lower-elevation villages, might also have offered newly crowded neighbors a little privacy.

At Old Caves, people sank small, vertical entrance holes into the hill slope and then hollowed out much larger chambers in the cinders below.

Before about 1250, most people in the high-elevation country east of the San Francisco Peaks lived in hamlets of one to several families, farming small plots of land nearby. Neighbors and kin lived not far away, and each hamlet formed part of a larger community that came together now and then for worship, marriage, and trade. As time went by, communities grew, but people's dwellings remained scattered. Exceptions to this pattern, such as Wupatki, Citadel, Elden, and Turkey Hill Pueblos and the cliff rooms at Walnut Canyon, were rare.

Toward the mid-1200s, something disrupted the old pattern of residence throughout the Sierra Sin Agua. Near O'Neill Crater, people rapidly left the Rio de Flag Valley. Some may have left the area entirely, but many took up residence on the slopes of the area's largest and most rugged nearby volcano, O'Neill Crater. There they built new pueblo and pit house structures, some at the very summit of the volcano and others on a relatively flat bench just below.

Individually, the post-1250 house groups at

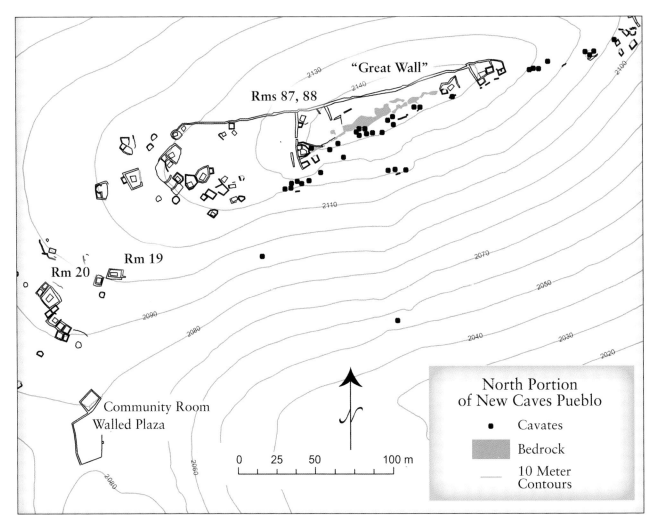

Figure 20.4. The north portion of New Caves, showing the "great wall" on the north. The steep slope to the southeast leads down into the volcanic crater.

Still, living conditions were difficult. Topping everything off, New Caves sat far above the farmland and water of the Rio de Flag Valley. Its residents, though no doubt physically fit, needed 20 to 30 minutes of strenuous exercise to climb up or down the hill carrying wood, food, and water.

Why would people tolerate such shortcomings? For hundreds of years, Hisat'sinom of the Sierra Sin Agua chose not to live in this place, and when they finally did, they stayed only briefly. We believe they did so in order to defend themselves against possible attack. When all things are considered, the only real advantage to living at New Caves was that the site could easily be fortified.

The earliest residents built a group of well-defended rooms on the highest peak. On the inner side of the peak, looking down into the crater, sheer cliffs of ragged lava and steep slopes of loose debris are unassailable. On the gentler north slope, a wall surrounds the upper rooms and extends from them 245 yards down the ridge of the mountain. People put a lot of effort into building this wall, sweating in the sun to move boulders weighing hundreds of pounds. The final breastwork stood two large rocks thick and at least chest high. With the wall blocking access from the north, the normal route to the village must have been up a steep trail on the west that leads to the saddle of the mountain. There, to enter the village, one had to pass through a walled plaza and past the village's community room.

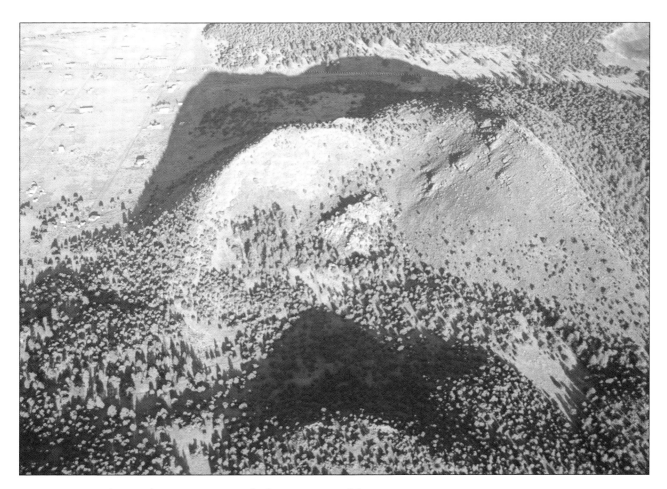

Figure 20.5. Aerial view of New Caves Crater, looking west toward features at summit.

Although the summit rooms were well built, they held few artifacts—roughly one-tenth the number of potsherds and other finds from comparable rooms in the lower parts of the site—suggesting that people spent little time in them. Perhaps the summit saw use as a refuge only once or occasionally, and most of the actual living took place a bit later and in lower parts of the site.

How real was the threat? The few sites in the Sierra Sin Agua with burned rooms and bodies showing signs of violent injury seem to be related to a brief flare-up of hostilities in the early 1100s (see chapter 10), long before the founding of New Caves. Otherwise, evidence for pervasive warfare in the Sierra Sin Agua is scant. We do not know who the aggressors of the late 1200s might have been, or why they threatened their neighbors. But violence need not have been common to justify our judgment that New Caves was built for defense. As

recent American history shows, it takes just a few dramatic events to change the outlook and politics of an entire people.

With a bit of imagination, we can envision the way fear among the residents of New Caves might have affected their lives. A time of disruption and movement brings anxiety and unhappiness. If outsiders or hostile neighbors actually raided New Caves, then the people suffered even more. The crowded conditions there likely exaggerated social tensions among villagers. Travel and trade had to be limited, making it harder to instruct children in their agricultural tasks, religious roles, and social obligations. If it was risky to stray far from the village, then it became more difficult to get water, collect wild plants, and cultivate crops.

The terrain around New Caves was always difficult to farm without irrigation, and the 1200s were a particularly hard time. According to tree-ring studies, this was a remarkably cool century, with no warm periods. The years spanning 1225 to 1245 and 1258 to 1271 were especially chilly. Droughts hit the area from 1215 through 1221 and again from 1292 to 1300. These conditions would have made high-elevation agriculture, already marginal, even more precarious, and in some years crops probably failed. By the late 1200s, people could no longer count on their neighbors to help out in difficult years. Some had moved away from adjacent areas such as Wupatki earlier in the 1200s, disrupting trade patterns and removing an important part of the social safety net.

In the face of these environmental and social hardships, the successful but carefully balanced agriculture of the Sierra Sin Agua might no longer have met the needs of a large population. One response to failing crops is conflict—desperate people begin to take from those who were formerly friends or neighbors. We believe that either internal conflict or raiders from equally troubled areas nearby drove Hisat'sinom residents from their peaceful hamlets to a fortified acropolis at New Caves and a similar setting at Old Caves.

But recall that only two of the four large, late sites in the Sierra Sin Agua were built atop volcanoes. Why didn't the people at Elden and Turkey Hill Pueblos, which lay in open, flat areas, also move to fortified places? First, not everyone behaves the same way in times of crisis. Second, these sites had grown large before the mid-1200s and so perhaps had no need of the protection afforded by the slopes of a volcano. Large, multi-story pueblos might already have been defensible, offering both large fighting forces and the threat of organized retaliation to any attack. Like Wupatki Pueblo earlier, Turkey Hill and Elden Pueblos had no ground-floor exterior doors, another possible defensive measure.

While most people gathered in defensible villages from the mid-1200s onward, a minority continued to live in small hamlets. A few of these were fortified and sat in defensible locations, but others lay in the open and show no signs of fortification. Most remain unexcavated, and we cannot date

them well enough to judge between two alternative scenarios. Did everyone respond to a single moment of crisis, after which attitudes softened and people returned to more scattered hamlets? Or did some people refuse to join the larger villages, choosing instead to take their chances in existing homes, hoping for the best or trying to defend themselves in place?

We suspect that life in the Sierra Sin Agua in the late 1200s ultimately proved unbearable. The loss of Wupatki and many other communities in the early 1200s, conflict and movement in the mid- to late 1200s, and the cumulative effects of drought and cold throughout the century broke the carefully developed system that supported human settlements in the region. Successful farming depended on each family's easy access to scattered pockets of good land. A larger community, far from its fields and fearing for its security, could not survive for long.

We will never fully know the drama of these last days at New Caves, but we can imagine the crop failures and hungry children, the looming threat of real or anticipated attacks, the difficulty of coping with moves and new neighbors living close by, and the need for courage and faith when the gods seemed to have abandoned the people. When the time finally came to leave, perhaps the residents of New Caves understood their migration to a new place as a necessary step in fulfilling prophesies that foretold such hard and painful times. Only a few generations after people built them, the houses at New Caves stood empty as their inhabitants joined even larger communities on Anderson Mesa, along the Little Colorado River, and at the Hopi Mesas. In coming years, other struggles would await the Hisat'sinom and their descendants, but they would happen in new homes and new lands, far from the volcanoes of the Sierra Sin Agua.

John C. Whittaker is a professor of anthropology at Grinnell College in Iowa. With Kathryn Kamp, he has been working in the Sierra Sin Agua since 1984. His other interests include prehistoric technology, especially experiments with flint knapping and atlatls.

Suggested Reading

Note: Master's theses from Northern Arizona University are available from many libraries through interlibrary loan.

Acord, Kenny
2005   "A Ceramic Inventory and Chronological Analysis of Sinagua Settlement at Walnut Canyon National Monument." Master's thesis, Department of Anthropology, Northern Arizona University, Flagstaff.

Balenquah, Lyle J.
2008   "Beyond Stone and Mortar: A Hopi Perspective on the Preservation of Ruins (and Culture)." *Heritage Management*, vol. 1, no. 2, pp. 145–162.

Brown, Gregory B.
1996   "Direct Crop Production: Evidence from Prehistoric Agricultural Fields." Master's thesis, Department of Anthropology, Northern Arizona University, Flagstaff.

Colton, Harold S.
1946   *The Sinagua: A Summary of the Archaeology of the Region of Flagstaff, Arizona.* Museum of Northern Arizona Bulletin 22. Northern Arizona Society of Science and Art, Flagstaff.
1953   *Potsherds: An Introduction to the Study of Prehistoric Southwestern Ceramics and Their Use in Historic Reconstruction.* Museum of Northern Arizona Bulletin 25. Northern Arizona Society of Science and Art, Flagstaff.

Dean, Jeffrey S.
2009   "One Hundred Years of Dendroarchaeology: Dating, Human Behavior, and Past Climate." In *Tree-Rings, Kings, and Old World Archaeology and Environment: Papers Presented in Honor of Peter Ian Kuniholm*, edited by Stuart W. Manning and Mary Jaye Bruce, pp. 25–31. Oxbow Press, Oxford, U.K.

Duffield, Wendell A., with photographs by Michael Collier
1998   *Volcanoes of Northern Arizona.* Grand Canyon Association Press, Flagstaff.

Elson, Mark D., editor
2006   *Sunset Crater Archaeology: The History of a Volcanic Landscape.* Center for Desert Archaeology, Tucson, Arizona.

Folb, Lisa
1996   "Cotton Fabrics and Wupatki Pueblo." Master's thesis, Department of Anthropology, Northern Arizona University, Flagstaff.

Garcia, Daniel
2004   "Prehistoric Ceramic Boundaries in the Flagstaff Region of Northern Arizona." Master's thesis, Department of Anthropology, Northern Arizona University, Flagstaff.

Hedquist, Saul L.
2007   "Inferring Sinagua Social Complexity: An Examination of the Quantity and Distribution of Exotic Material Goods." Master's thesis, Department of Anthropology, Northern Arizona University, Flagstaff.

Jones, Courtney Reeder
1995   *Letters from Wupatki.* Edited by Lisa Rapoport. University of Arizona Press, Tucson.

Kamp, Kathryn A.

1998   *Life in the Pueblo: Understanding the Past through Archaeology.* Waveland Press, Prospect Heights, Illinois.

Kamp, Kathryn A., and John C. Whittaker

1999   *Surviving Adversity: The Sinagua of Lizard Man Village.* University of Utah Press, Salt Lake City.

Lamb, Susan

1995   *Wupatki National Monument.* Western National Parks Association, Tucson, Arizona.

Lambert, Ruth E.

2005   "Investigations of Small Structures in the Citadel District of Wupatki National Monument." Ph.D. dissertation, University of New Mexico, Albuquerque.

McGregor, John C.

1941   *Winona and Ridge Ruin, Part 1: Architecture and Material Culture.* Museum of Northern Arizona Bulletin 18. Northern Arizona Society of Science and Art, Flagstaff.

Murphy, Tracy L.

2000   "Ornamentation and Social Affinity: Shell Ornaments and the Hohokam Influence at Winona Village." Master's thesis, Department of Anthropology, Northern Arizona University, Flagstaff.

Nash, Stephen E.

1999   *Time, Trees, and Prehistory: Tree-Ring Dating and the Development of North American Archaeology, 1914–1950.* University of Utah Press, Salt Lake City.

Novotny, Michael J.

2007   "Reading between the Sites: A Spatial-Analytical Examination of Off-Site and On-Site Projectile Points." Master's thesis, Department of Anthropology, Northern Arizona University, Flagstaff.

Olson, Alan P.

1966   "Split-Twig Figurines from NA 5607, Northern Arizona." *Plateau* (Museum of Northern Arizona), vol. 38, no. 3, pp. 55–61.

Pilles, Peter J., Jr.

1996   "The Pueblo III Period along the Mogollon Rim: The Honanki, Elden, and Turkey Hill Phases of the Sinagua." In *The Prehistoric Pueblo World, A.D. 1150–1350,* edited by Michael A. Adler, pp. 59–72. University of Arizona Press, Tucson.

Salzer, Matthew

2007   "Dendroclimatic Reconstructions and Paleoenvironmental Analyses for the U.S. 89 Project Area." In *Sunset Crater Archaeology: The History of a Volcanic Landscape,* edited by Mark D. Elson, pp. 103–131. Center for Desert Archaeology, Tucson, Arizona.

Schofer, Jeanne Stevens

2006   "Foundations of Cultural Landscape: Mobility and Settlement Strategies at Wupatki National Monument, AD 1065–1160." Master's thesis, Department of Anthropology, Northern Arizona University, Flagstaff.

Smith, Watson

1952   *Excavations in Big Hawk Valley, Wupatki National Monument, Arizona.* Museum of Northern Arizona Bulletin 24. Northern Arizona Society of Science and Art, Flagstaff.

Teague, Lynn S.

1998   *Textiles in Southwestern Prehistory.* University of New Mexico Press, Albuquerque.

Thybony, Scott, with photographs by George H. H. Huey

1987   *Fire and Stone: A Road Guide to Wupatki and Sunset Crater National Monuments.* Western National Parks Association, Tucson, Arizona.

Picture Credits

Abbreviations

MNA	Museum of Northern Arizona
NAU	Northern Arizona University
USC	University of Southern California

Color section, after page 48: Plates 1–3, 13, 16–18, 20–22, and 24–30, photos by Dan Boone and Ryan Belnap, Bilby Research Center, NAU. Plate 4 (2009), courtesy Bern Carey, photographer. Plates 5 and 7 (2009), courtesy Joseph P. Vogel, photographer. Plate 6, photo by Josef Muench, between 1950 and 1970, courtesy NAU Cline Library, NAU.PH.2003.11.23.M6892. Plates 8 (Jan. 1985), 9 (Nov. 2004), and 12 (Aug. 1985), photos by Peter J. Pilles Jr., courtesy Coconino National Forest. Plate 10, photo by Evelyn Billo and Robert Mark, Aug. 1999, courtesy Rupestrian CyberServices (http://www.rupestrian.com). Plate 11, illustration by Victor O. Leshyk (http://victorleshyk.com/), based on original photography by Dan Boone and Ryan Belnap, Bilby Research Center, NAU, and Christian E. Downum. Plate 14, illustration by Victor O. Leshyk, based on 3-D lidar scan data provided by Western Mapping, Inc., and original photography by Boone, Belnap, and Downum. Plates 15 and 23, illustration by Victor O. Leshyk, based on original photography by Boone and Belnap and concept by Downum. Plate 19 (2009), courtesy Christian E. Downum, photographer.

Front matter: Maps 1–4 by Victor O. Leshyk.

Chapter One: Fig. 1.1 (Jan. 1969), courtesy Peter J. Pilles Jr., photographer. Fig. 1.2, photo by Peter J. Pilles Jr., May 1994, courtesy Coconino National Forest.

Chapter Two: Fig. 2.1, photo by Peter J. Pilles Jr., Sept. 1981, courtesy Coconino National Forest. Fig. 2.2, map by Victor O. Leshyk.

Chapter Three: Figs. 3.1 and 3.4, photo by Dan Boone and Ryan Belnap, Bilby Research Center, NAU. Fig. 3.2, courtesy Lyle Balenquah, photographer. Fig. 3.3, photo by Charles C. Pierce, about 1901, courtesy USC Digital Archives, CHS-1064.

Chapter Four: Figs. 4.1, 4.2, 4.4, 4.5, and 4.6, photos by Evelyn Billo and Robert Mark, 1999–2008, courtesy Rupestrian CyberServices. Fig. 4.3, illustration by Victor O. Leshyk. Fig. 4.7, illustration by Jane Kolber, courtesy Donald E. Weaver Jr. Fig. 4.8 by Donald E. Weaver Jr., Plateau Mountain Desert Research, 1997.

Chapter Five: Fig. 5.1, photo by Peter J. Pilles Jr., May 1994, courtesy Coconino National Forest. Figs. 5.2, 5.3, and 5.6, illustrations by Victor O. Leshyk. Fig. 5.4, photographer unknown, courtesy MNA (NA1920B.9). Fig. 5.5, courtesy Michael Collier, photographer.

Chapter Six: Fig. 6.1, photographer unknown, 1928, courtesy Laboratory of Tree-Ring Research. Fig. 6.2, photo by Dan Boone and Ryan Belnap, Bilby Research Center, NAU. Figs. 6.3 and 6.7, illustrations by Victor O. Leshyk; fig. 6.7 based on original illustration by Matthew Salzer. Figs. 6.4 (Dec. 1985) and 6.6 (Oct. 1976), photos by Peter J. Pilles Jr., courtesy Coconino National Forest. Fig. 6.5, illustration by Ryan Belnap, adapted from original figure by Matthew Salzer, courtesy Desert Archaeology, Inc., Tucson.

Chapter Seven: Fig. 7.1, courtesy John Running, photographer. Fig. 7.2, illustration by Victor O. Leshyk. Fig. 7.3 (May 2009), courtesy Christian E. Downum, photographer. Fig. 7.4, photo by Dan Boone and Ryan Belnap, Bilby Research Center, NAU. Fig. 7.5, courtesy MNA (E-200.87.009).

Chapter Eight: Fig. 8.1, illustration by Victor O. Leshyk. Figs. 8.2, 8.3, 8.4, 8.5, 8.6, and 8.7, photos by Dan Boone and Ryan Belnap, Bilby Research Center, NAU.

Chapter Nine: Figs. 9.1 top, courtesy Peter J. Pilles Jr., photographer. Fig. 9.1 bottom, courtesy MNA (NA1785.42, inset NA1785.124). Fig. 9.2, photo by Peter J. Pilles Jr., May 1978, courtesy Coconino National Forest. Fig. 9.3, illustration by Victor O. Leshyk, based on 1999 map by James P. Holmlund, Western Mapping, Inc., Tucson. Figs. 9.4, 9.5, 9.7, 9.8, and 9.9, photos by Dan Boone and Ryan Belnap, Bilby Research Center, NAU. Fig. 9.6, courtesy MNA (NA1785.10).

Chapter Ten: Fig. 10.1, photo by Dan Boone and Ryan Belnap, Bilby Research Center, NAU. Fig. 10.2, photographer unknown, probably E. J. Hands, courtesy Christian E. Downum. Figs. 10.3 and 10.7, photos by John C. McGregor, about 1930 and 1935, respectively, courtesy Christian E. Downum. Fig. 10.4, photographer unknown, 1940s, courtesy MNA (MS-207-2009). Figs. 10.5 and 10.6, maps by Harold S. Colton, 1946 and 1939, respectively, courtesy MNA. Figs. 10.8 and 10.9, maps by Victor O. Leshyk.

Chapter Eleven: Fig. 11.1, photo by Peter J. Pilles Jr., June 1982, courtesy Coconino National Forest. Fig. 11.2, illustration by Laurie Coveney-Thom, based on original 1934 drawing by J. C. Fisher Motz. Fig. 11.3, illustration by Victor O. Leshyk, based on 1999 map by James P. Holmlund, Western Mapping, Inc., Tucson, Arizona. Fig. 11.4, photo by Cooper Aerial Photo, Inc., courtesy U.S. National Park Service. Fig. 11.5, photo by Dan Boone and Ryan Belnap, Bilby Research Center, NAU. Fig. 11.6, courtesy MNA (NA405NorthUnit.5).

Chapter Twelve: Fig. 12.1, photo by Edward S. Curtis, courtesy NAU Cline Library, Edward S. Curtis Collection, NAU.PH.93.38.4. Figs. 12.2, 12.3, and 12.7, photos by Charles C. Pierce, about 1900, courtesy USC Digital Archives, CHS-3682, CHS-3361, and CHS-3706, respectively. Figs. 12.4, 12.5, and 12.6, photos by Dan Boone and Ryan Belnap, Bilby Research Center, NAU.

Chapter Thirteen: Figs. 13.1, 13.3, and 13.4, reproduced from Victor Mindeleff and Cosmos Mindeleff, *A Study of Pueblo Architecture: Tusayan and Cibola*, Eighth Annual Report of the Bureau of Ethnology, 1886–1887 (Washington, D.C.: Government Printing Office, 1891). Fig. 13.2, photo by Peter J. Pilles Jr., Oct. 1983, courtesy Coconino National Forest. Fig. 13.5 (1982–84), courtesy Christian E. Downum, photographer. Fig. 13.6, photo by Dan Boone and Ryan Belnap, Bilby Research Center, NAU.

Chapter Fourteen: Fig. 14.1, photo by Charles C. Pierce, about 1900, courtesy USC Digital Archives, CHS-1033. Fig. 14.2, photo by Monty Roessel, 1999, courtesy U.S. National Park Service. Figs. 14.3, 14.4, and 14.8, illustrations by Harold S. Colton, about 1932, 1931, and 1931, respectively, courtesy MNA. Fig. 14.5, photo by Josef Muench, between 1950 and 1970, courtesy NAU Cline Library, NAU.PH.2003.11.23.L1665. Figs. 14.6 (April 1969) and 14.7 (Sept. 1972), courtesy Peter J. Pilles Jr., photographer.

Chapter Fifteen: Figs. 15.1 and 15.5, photos by Dan Boone and Ryan Belnap, Bilby Research Center, NAU; scale model in fig. 15.5 constructed by Christian E. Downum. Figs. 15.2 (Aug. 2010), 15.3 (June 1984), and 15.4 (Feb. 1993), courtesy Christian E. Downum, photographer.

Chapter Sixteen: Fig. 16.1 (June 1994), courtesy Christian E. Downum, photographer. Figs. 16.2 and 16.3, illustrations by Victor O. Leshyk, after original map and original concept, respectively, by Gregory B. Brown. Fig. 16.4, photo by William H. Jackson, about 1875, courtesy Colorado Historical Society.

Chapter Seventeen: Fig. 17.1, photo by Edward S. Curtis, about 1906, courtesy NAU Cline Library, NAU.PH.93.38.24. Figs. 17.2, 17.3, 17.4, 17.5 top right, 17.6, and 17.7, photos by Dan Boone and Ryan Belnap, Bilby Research Center, NAU. Fig. 17.5 left, courtesy Christian E. Downum; center right, courtesy Arizona State Museum (ASM 1415); bottom, courtesy Christian Downum, photographer, photo taken June 1994.

Chapter Eighteen: Fig. 18.1, photo by Charles C. Pierce, around 1898, courtesy USC Digital Archives, CHS-4574. Figs. 18.2, 18.4, and 18.5, photos by Dan Boone and Ryan Belnap, Bilby Research Center, NAU. Fig. 18.3, illustration by Victor O. Leshyk, from original drawing by Lisa Folb. Fig. 18.6, photo of shirt courtesy Arizona State Museum (ASM 67557); insets of cloth fragments, photos by Dan Boone and Ryan Belnap, Bilby Research Center, NAU.

Chapter Nineteen: Figs. 19.1, 19.3, and 19.5, photos by Dan Boone and Ryan Belnap, Bilby Research Center, NAU. Fig. 19.2, illustration by Victor O. Leshyk, from a 1941 map by Harold S. Colton. Fig. 19.4, photo by Charles C. Pierce, about 1901, courtesy USC Digital Archives, CHS-1028.

Chapter Twenty: Figs. 20.1 and 20.3 (both 2006), courtesy John C. Whittaker, photographer. Figs. 20.2 and 20.4, illustrations by Victor O. Leshyk, from original drawings by Kathryn Kamp, courtesy Coconino National Forest. Fig. 20.5 by Peter J. Pilles Jr., courtesy Coconino National Forest.

Other illustrations: *Half-title page (p. i) and p. 5*, anthropomorphic petroglyph from Picture Canyon. Photo by Evelyn Billo and Robert Mark. Courtesy Billo and Mark. Drawn by Victor O. Leshyk. *Title page (p. iii)*, birds perched on spiral petroglyph from Wupatki National Monument. Taken from "Wupatki Rock Art," by Bruce A. Anderson, in *The Wupatki Archaeological Inventory Survey Project: Final Report* (1990), compiled by B.A. Anderson, U.S. National Park Service, Southwest Cultural Resources Center, Professional Paper No. 35, Santa Fe. Courtesy U.S. National Park Service. Re-drawn by Victor O. Leshyk. *Contents (p. v)*, bighorn sheep petroglyph from Wupatki National Monument. Taken from "Wupatki Rock Art," by Bruce A. Anderson, in *The Wupatki Archaeological Inventory Survey Project: Final Report* (1990), compiled by B. A. Anderson, U.S. National Park Service, Southwest Cultural Resources Center, Professional Paper No. 35, Santa Fe. Courtesy U.S. National Park Service. Re-drawn by Victor O. Leshyk. *Contents (p. vi), p. 86, and p. 147*, Tusayan White Ware pottery designs drawn by Julian D. Hayden, 1934. Courtesy Christian E. Downum. *Second half-title page (p. xv) and p. 25*, mountain lion (petroglyph) from Crack-in-Rock Pueblo, Wupatki National Monument. Photo by Donald E. Weaver Jr. Courtesy Weaver. Drawn by Victor O. Leshyk. *Pages 9 and 95*, interlocking connected square spirals petroglyph from Picture Canyon. Photo by Evelyn Billo and Robert Mark. Courtesy Billo and Mark. Drawn by Victor O. Leshyk. *Page 49*, group of people holding hands (petroglyph) from Chavez Pass. From illustration by Jane Kolber. Courtesy Kolber. Re-drawn by Victor O. Leshyk. *Page 77*, horned figure (possibly a Kokopelli) petroglyph, from Wupatki National Monument. Taken from "Wupatki Rock Art," by Bruce A. Anderson, in *The Wupatki Archaeological Inventory Survey Project: Final Report* (1990), compiled by B.A. Anderson, U.S. National Park Service, Southwest Cultural Resources Center, Professional Paper No. 35, Santa Fe. Courtesy U.S. National Park Service. Re-drawn by Victor O. Leshyk. *Page 87*, complex abstract life form petroglyph from Chavez Pass. From illustration by Jane Kolber. Courtesy Kolber. Re-drawn by Victor O. Leshyk. *Page 103*, coiled snake petroglyph from near Wupatki Pueblo. Taken from "Wupatki Rock Art," by Bruce A. Anderson, in *The Wupatki Archaeological Inventory Survey Project: Final Report* (1990), compiled by B. A. Anderson, U.S. National Park Service, Southwest Cultural Resources Center, Professional Paper No. 35, Santa Fe. Courtesy U.S. National Park Service. Re-drawn by Victor O. Leshyk. *Page 117*, Complex geometric form petroglyph, from Picture Canyon. Photo by Evelyn Billo and Robert Mark. Courtesy Billo and Mark. Drawn by Victor O. Leshyk. *Page 155*, Footprint (human or bear), Anderson Mesa. Photo by Donald E. Weaver Jr. Courtesy Weaver. Drawn by Victor O. Leshyk.

Index

Numbers printed in *italics* refer to illustrations; numbers beginning with uppercase P refer to plates; numbers printed in **bold** refer to maps.